The Joey Boots Chronicles

The Joey Boots Chronicles

with Scott Zeif

ISBN: 0692948120
ISBN 13: 9780692948125
Library of Congress Control Number: 2017914337
ZTrainShuttle, New Rochelle, NY

TABLE OF CONTENTS

Dear Reader,

The following are stories compiled from the life of Joey Boots. Joey Boots was a regular caller and contributor to the Howard Stern Radio Show.

I was at a bar one night when I heard Joey's familiar voice behind me, and instantly recognized it from the radio. We became friends, chatted on AOL Instant Messenger; he bought me weed and offered blowjobs, which I declined.

During our chats and hangouts, Joey began sharing anecdotes from his past. Some really compelling stories about his life and brushes with fame. Then we got the idea to put these stories together in a book. So Joey started talking, emailing and writing on legal pads, while I interviewed, transcribed and found a narrative.

But after all this, we never got around to putting these chronicles out. So here's the story of Joey Boots, in his words and voice. The names of non-public figures, including his real last name, have been changed at the request of Joey.

- *Scott Zeif*

*Dedicated to Howard Stern -
saint and savior, god and goddess.*

CHAPTER 1

GROWING UP BOOTS

Let's just start at the fucking beginning. It's a very good place to start. Some nun in a musical once told me that. I think it was Whoopi Goldberg.

My real name is Joseph Bootsolino. That's where my nickname Joey Boots comes from. That's the first secret I'll reveal. Want to hear a few more? This is the first and only time I'm sharing a lot of this with anyone. Will anyone care? Well someone has to care at some point, right? Those are the laws of below averages.

You remember that book *A Million Little Pieces* by James Frey that was featured on Oprah Winfrey's Book Club? It was all about this guy's crazy drug-fueled life. But it turned out he embellished a lot of that stuff to make it seem better and more exciting. Then Oprah got pissed and brought him back on her show to yell at him.

I'm like, "This guy wrote a book? I could write a book." I lived 10 times this guy's life and he had to make half the shit up.

Now I find myself in a Yonkers sober home with a bunch of kids playing handball on the other side of my bedroom wall. I was young once.

I was born on May 24, 1967 at Our Lady of Mercy Hospital in the Bronx. On birthday zero, my 18-year-old mom sent me to the Angel Guardian Home for orphans. I was the second boy she had and then sent to that same orphanage. She was a prolific producer of unwanted white babies.

Vincent and Sofia Bootsolino were a young Italian couple from Long Island. They adopted their first boy from the Angel Guardian Home two years before. When I became available, the nuns who ran the orphanage called the Bootsolinos and asked if they wanted another boy from the same exact birth mother, but with different fathers. They jumped at the chance to get their son's true half-brother.

And that was me. Joey Boots. Hello.

They took me back to their home in Massapequa, a small suburban hamlet on Long Island. The whole town is just about 4 square miles. My parents ended up having one more son naturally - my little brother Frankie.

A lot of famous people are from Massapequa. Jerry Seinfeld, the Baldwin brothers, the Stray Cats, Christine Jorgensen (first person in the US to have a sex change operation), Steve Guttenberg, Jessica Hahn, Stuttering John Melendez, Joey Buttafuoco and gangster Carlo Gambino.

There were lots of happy times growing up. We went to Disney for my 7th birthday, summer resorts in the Poconos, animal farms, zoos and amusement parks. We did all that.

Our middle-class neighborhood was full of kids. Hockey in the driveways, roller-skating and sports played on the streets and fields. It was like the beginning of a car commercial. Sprinklers hitting kids on bikes and all that shit.

But I was a fat kid. Or "husky" like the clothes section said. I wasn't athletic and didn't have much interest or talent in sports. So I sought out other hobbies. I soon found my calling in pulling pranks. Messing with people in funny ways and making their day just a little more frustrating and annoying.

At the end of our block there was a fence between the street and Long Island Expressway. In the winter my friends and I would cut a hole in the fence and pummel cars with snowballs. These guys were going well over 60 mph. Some of them would get off at the next exit and try to find us. But they never would.

Ring and run - ringing doorbells and running away - was also big in my neighborhood, but we got carried away. One night we took a dead possum, put lighter fluid on it and hung it from someone's front porch. Then we set it ablaze and dashed away. The guy opened his door and freaked the fuck out. After that we stopped doing that prank, afraid someone would have a heart attack.

So there were good times. But I mostly felt out of place. Growing up adopted, I felt left out and resentful of my adopted parents. I know, "Boo-hoo." I was adopted. But to a kid it can be a big deal.

The Bootsolinos were very Catholic. My mom was a Long Island stay-at-home housewife and my dad was a cop in the county where we lived.

When I was young, I think I was content. But things felt worse when I got a little older and wanted to express myself and be an individual. You get to an age when you want to do your own thing, but I wasn't allowed to. It seemed that all our friends' parents gave them more freedom as they got older while mine clamped down. They could all stay out later than my brothers and I could. My dad always dictated exactly how I should style my hair (parted to the side, not the middle) and the kinds of shirts I could wear (rock concert shirts were a no-no). I couldn't make any decisions on my own.

And when they did allow us out at night, our parents made my older brother Vinnie and me wear these big bright orange hunting jackets – hunting vests! They said this was so a car would see us clearly and not hit us. Can you imagine the ridicule we got from our friends when we showed up in bright orange hunting gear in the middle of the Long Island suburbs? So we started ditching the jackets in bushes and retrieved them later. My brother and I would freeze our asses off all night just to avoid feeling embarrassed in front of our friends.

My dad installed a giant bell on our front porch. When he wanted us home, he would ring it loudly. This was the suburbs – not a fucking farm! And all the kids would tease us shouting, "There's the bell. Time for the cows to go home," and start *mooing*.

These kids would never say shit like that when my father was around. Our friends were scared of my father because not only was he a cop, but when they came over he grilled them like a cop. He was very harsh with them and me.

In the middle of a store, my father would have no qualms about smacking me real hard across the face and yelling at me at the top of his lungs if I aggravated him. I'd look around and the other people would be watching in horror. I hoped someone would run over, save me, take me away from him or just do something. But nobody ever said nothing dude. None of the store employees, no other people. They all just looked at me and probably felt sorry for me. And that always made me feel sorry for myself.

I grew up always feeling sorry for myself.

I was frequently lambasted, psychologically and physically abused by my father. He just scared the shit out of me when I would fuck up in any way. I would get smacked and chased around the house by my mother with a wooden spoon and cutting board, and my father with a belt, and I knew the windows were open and the neighbors could hear screaming and yelling. Later they'd ask if I was ok. Neighbors would talk shit about my father to me because they knew he was a maniac. I didn't argue.

I don't know if hate is the word, but I feared my father and wished we had a closer relationship like my friends had with theirs. I wanted the love of my father but never felt I had it. Yes, once he took me to see Doug Henning the magician at Radio City, which was a great day. But he never let me forget that we did this one thing.

I would fantasize that my father would be killed at work and one of the other cops would adopt me.

CHAPTER 2

JESUS SCHOOL

What do you have to do to get suspended in third grade? I'm glad you asked.

I was in Catholic school and my 3rd grade teacher was Mr. McPherson. He was this big ugly Irish dude. Must have weighed 350 pounds and stood like 6'5. He was as big as Beetlejuice thinks he is.

Our class was in the hallway standing in line waiting to go to an assembly. Then a kid standing a few students in front of me jumped out of line and flipped off the light switch, which was right next to me. Then the kid jumped back to his place in line. Mr. McPherson came over and started yelling at me for turning off the light. Grabbed me by my fucking ear and pulled me off the line.

Dude, I got so upset. My breathing got real fucking heavy and I started hyperventilating. I was crying hard and protesting, saying that I hadn't done anything. Someone else flipped off the light. He didn't listen and just dragged me into the class, berating me and smacking me on the head.

Once we got in class, I broke away from him. Then Mr. McPherson started chasing me. He was big and I was scared. All I could think to do was pick up one of those little plastic chairs we sat in and throw it at him. The chair hit him right on the head. The next thing I knew, my parents were picking me up from school. I was suspended.

And it all started with something I didn't even do dude. But that was me – playing the victim, getting into some shit then making things worse.

And that's how I always felt. I grew up with a victim mentality and wore it. Woe is me. I held on to that shit. I cried for too long. At first I think for legitimate reasons, but I held on to it for too long and let it affect me negatively.

That wasn't even the first time I was suspended. The first time was in Kindergarten.

Kindergarten man. My dad would pick me up from school in his cop car. I liked to sit in the back seat with my hands behind my back. Other kids would come to the window and ask what happened. I'd say I was under arrest and my father would play along.

One day in kindergarten, the whole class was making plastic bead necklaces. I called this kid Bobby over. I said, "Bobby, close your eyes and I'll give you a big surprise."

He stood there gleefully with his eyes squinted shut. I took one of the plastic marble beads and shoved it up his nose with my finger. And it went really far and tight into his nose.

Dude, it got stuck in his nose. He fucking freaked out, the teacher freaked out. They had to call an ambulance, take him to the hospital and have it surgically removed dude. It was that lodged in his nose.

I wasn't allowed back in school for a week. And when I did come back, this guy from the local ambulance corp. visited our class and talked about the dangers of playing pranks. He didn't mention me specifically, but everybody knew who he was talking about. The other kids looked, pointed at me and made that "mmm" sound. That "mmm" sound stayed in my head through life and would ring in my ear whenever I got caught doing something wrong.

I did have some good times in Catholic school. There was this great teacher Mrs. Greene who made me her class pet.

The Vietnam War just ended in the past few years, so there were a few Vietnamese kids at our school adopted by local families. Mrs. Greene gave me the job of helping the Vietnamese kids with English. I would take them all in a little group, read to them, show them pictures and pronounce words like house, dog, cat, cup and car. All important words for getting around in society. Then I had them repeat after me.

And I just remember this one Vietnamese kid I bonded with - Hoang Devon. I took a special liking to him because even though we couldn't speak each other's languages, it was just special. I got so much joy out of teaching and giving to someone else and it made me feel real good. Oddly enough after helping Hoang learn English, he did better on tests than me. But I still felt good.

That experience got me to start fantasizing about growing up and doing good things in the world. To become a Christian missionary and help people like I did in that class. That's what I wanted to do as a young kid. Somewhere along the line I took a different fucking path.

I wasn't a very popular kid in Catholic school. Kids would have birthday parties and I was the only one not invited. I felt really bad about it man. I felt woe is me. I became the loner you know? For some reason I was a loner and became comfortable being the loner. Maybe because I was sad all the time. It was a turnoff to people. I was easy to tease and make fun of and fuck with. Kids would tease me about being adopted after it came up in class. Then they would just fuck with me over different things like my weight and clothes.

At one point, I did have a really cool go-cart. It was made out of an ironing board, a milk box and some old baby carriage wheels. My dad helped me construct it and we used to push it down hills and ride it.

Tommy Barker, the most popular kid in school, started hanging out with me a lot. We'd go to each other's houses and ride my go-cart down the street. It felt great to finally have a real friend and spend time together.

After a couple months playing, I was at Tommy's house and it was a week before his birthday. I mentioned something about his party coming up, and he suddenly blew up at me. "You know the only reason I hang out with you is for your go-cart," he shouted. Then Tommy told me to go home and never come back.

That devastated me. Fucking devastated me. I withdrew even more. I became more of a loner and distrustful of all people and relationships.

And then cut to the middle of 7th grade. My class was in the boys' locker room changing at the end of gym class. Then somebody killed the lights. All I could remember next was dozens of kids just pummeling me from every direction like it was an organized fucking thing to beat the shit out of me and gang up against me.

The lights went back on. Then the gym teacher Mr. Bailey came in and shouted, "What's going on? Bootsolino! You causing trouble again? Get over to the principal's office now!"

I was all upset crying and couldn't even fucking talk. I was like what the fuck just happened? And there was no reason for it. Just kids being bullies you know? Meanwhile, I was the one in trouble.

I walked closer to the main office, still fuming and processing all this, not in my right mind. The principal and head nun, Sister Adine, stepped out in the hall, pointed at me and told me to get in her office right now. I just kept walking past her and said, "Fuck you!"

"What did you say, Mr. Bootsolino?"

"Fuck you. I ain't coming nowhere."

Sister Adine called my mother. I was hoping my mom would come in there and see how bruised and upset I was, ask for my side of the story and defend me. Instead she just signed me out and enrolled me in public school the next day.

CHAPTER 3

PUB

Do you want to read about me in public school? If not, go to the chapter about me fucking Lisa Lampanelli – that's a good one! Or do some other activity like braid your bunny rabbit.

So I started public school in the middle of 7th grade. I went from a school where no one liked me to a school where no one knew me. In my lonely and fractured social world, it was an upgrade.

The first thing that comes to mind is my 7th grade English teacher. The big rumor about her was that there was booze in her Sprite can, because she always reeked of alcohol and seemed to act tipsy.

Well this teacher was a single parent and lived with her young son. One night, her kid was at home watching a TV movie about Houdini. The magician did a trick where he hung from a hook with his hands tied and managed to escape. So her son tried that same trick. Our teacher found him hanging in the closet, lifeless.

She was out of school for two weeks. After we heard about what happened, all we did during the time she was out was play Hangman with the substitute teacher. And when our teacher did come back, there were hangmen all over the board. That was pretty fucked up. I just remember it was one of the cruelest things I ever did. And I took part in that. It haunts me to this day how mean-spirited and terrible that was.

When I entered public school, I really wanted to fit in like I never did in Catholic school. And the easiest and most fun way was through drugs and alcohol.

I started smoking weed with kids in 7th grade. I also began buying black beauties - strong caffeine pills popular with truckers in the 1970s and '80s. Black beauties were basically the precursor to meth and cost a dollar each.

Then I started selling drugs. I'd go to one of the black neighborhoods of Long Island and buy dime bags of weed. This was back in the early '80s when these $10 bags could roll you at least 18 joints. I'd sell 10 joints and keep 8 to smoke myself. Or I'd sell more joints and buy cigarettes. 55 cents a pack in those days.

Around the same time, I had my first drink at a backyard family party at our house. One of my uncles was a heavy drinker and convinced my mom to let me have one sip of beer. I was in love. I just remember feeling great. To me, drinking beer meant I was mature. I felt excited holding it, being seen holding it and above all - drinking it.

Now that I was allowed to have one sip and already had some beer on my breath, I figured no one at the party would notice if I had a few more. So throughout the day I snuck at least 20 beer cans up to my bedroom. I drank a couple and started getting a great buzz. The other cans I kept in a secret hiding spot to share with my friends later.

Drinking soon became an every weekend thing. When I was 14, I got a fake driver's license that said I was 21. Back then there weren't picture licenses. On your ID they only gave a description like your height, weight, eye color and such. So it was much easier to get a fake ID card and pass for older.

So I became the man with my friends since I could buy beer, and we didn't have to stand outside 7-Eleven and ask older kids who looked cool if they would buy it for us. On many occasions, my friends and I would break into local stores at night, take shopping carts full of beer and stash them at our friend's house, whose mom could give two shits what we did. She would even give us money to buy ourselves beer and pick her up a nickel bag of weed.

I was also socializing more and started hooking up with a girl for the first time. In the summer before high school,

I got with this chick named Erica from the neighborhood. She had huge tits and I loved to make out while grabbing her melons. She even let me feel her pussy. My older brother Vinnie hooked up with one of her friends on the grass nearby. Years later, I could have sworn I saw Erica on TV getting arrested on the first episode of *Cops*.

I was having lots of fun with Erica exploring and enjoying my first up-close looks at a girl's body. But by that time, I was also getting pretty nervous and confused about sex.

Around the age of 11-12, I was staying over at my neighbor friend Jimmy's house. We were sleeping in the same bed as we'd done so many sleepovers before. I don't know what made me think to do this, but I moved my leg so it touched his leg, but only slightly. He didn't move his leg away.

Then I moved my leg a little closer, pressing harder against Jimmy's leg. Again he did nothing. I then moved my hand and brushed it against his waist and he stayed still. I slowly moved closer every minute or two until my hand was on his stomach. He stayed still and didn't stop me. Then I slowly worked my hand down into his jammies to find a fully erect penis!

I put my hand on it and played with him for a little while. Neither of us said anything. He reached for my penis, which was fully hard as well, and played with mine.

Now I might have been young, but I knew from porno magazines and talking with other kids what a blowjob was and knew what I wanted to do. I got under the covers, took his penis into my mouth and sucked it. I took it out and licked it all over. I paused and told him not to cum in my mouth because I was scared how it would taste.

When Jimmy was ready to cum, he pulled out and shot his load right into my face. Feeling the warmth of it turned me on and I took some on my finger and tasted it with the tip of my tongue.

"Salty," I thought. From that point on, I knew I was not like other boys.

I started having dreams of being with boys in the classic boyfriend/girlfriend sense, and thought this was very weird and wrong. Something that must forever be kept secret from everyone. I played the part of liking girls throughout school and talked the talk with the guys.

Even though I wasn't enrolled in Catholic school anymore, my mother was still very religious and wanted me to hang out with Father Sebastian. He was this young hip priest from the church. My mother and I both thought he was a really nice guy. So I started talking to him, especially when I was having trouble with my parents.

One afternoon, Father Sebastian was driving me home from church. He started asking me questions like, "Are you having sex yet?" I said a little. I was 13. He asked if I was using condoms, because they were against the Catholic Church.

Then he asked if I wanted him to show me how to put a condom on. He was touching himself through his pants.

I said, "No, that's alright man. I know how to do it."

As we pulled up to my house, Father Sebastian told me any time I wanted to talk he was there, and it would be our secret. I got out of the car and again he asked, "Are you sure you don't want anything?"

"Five dollars," I said, which he gave me then took off.

Here I was - a kid with gay feelings. And I even managed to fuck up getting molested. Now look at all these people suing and making millions. I could be rich now and gotten into some hot scenes with the Father.

In high school, I started hanging out with a bunch of the clicker Jewish kids. In school they called them the Jewish Mafia and I was the one goy in the group. I thought all the guys in that crowd were so cool, nice, fun, and…. hot.

My best friend, and the hottest of the hot Jews, was Nathan Pasternak. We became tight friends. I would stay over his house on weekends for sleepovers, though we rarely slept. What was great about being there was that Nathan's parents actually encouraged us to stay up all night and make prank calls. Then they would laugh about our exploits in the morning. I was in heaven there and thought his parents were the coolest ones around. Mine would never allow something like that.

Nathan and I used to prank our 9th grade teacher Mr. Haverstock, who hosted the *Homework Helper* show on the local cable station. We called in during his show and fucked with this guy, calling him Mr. Have-a-cock, dropping F-bombs and fucking with him about being bald, saying crazy shit. It was our first time doing live prank phone calls. Hardcore man. They had no video delay to censor the curses or even caller ID on that channel. They couldn't drop shit, they had nothing man. I wish to this day I could get those tapes cause that was some funny shit.

And at school, Mr. Haverstock would try to figure out who called the show and disrespected him the night before. He always suspected my crew of guys cause we were always fucking with him. But he couldn't prove shit, which made it more funny to us and more frustrating to him. I'd like to call him all these years later and admit it was me. He's probably pretty old now.

Nathan would often talk about girls he liked. He was a really good looking guy with a swimmer's body and very developed pecs. I was very much turned on by him, but didn't dare let him know my feelings. I would go to sleep and dream of him, think about doing fun things, and just being around him made me feel really happy and fulfilled. I wanted to kiss him, run my hands across his body and cuddle with him on the couch while we watched movies.

This started my infatuation with Jewish guys. Going into high school I hung with Nathan Pasternak, Brian Berger, Mike Katz and Matt Korngold. I went to all their Bar Mitzvahs and ate Passover dinner at their houses. Read from the Haggadah and all that.

I dared not tell my friends (whose true friendship I cherished most of all) that I was attracted to them and fantasized about each one while masturbating at home. I was a frequent masturbator. I did this mostly by dry humping the couch or my bed, then using my hand or fist to apply pressure against as I ground my penis into it, and came in my underwear.

My poor mother had to know what I was doing behind those closed doors as she cleaned my underwear, but thankfully never said anything. I think she was either really embarrassed to say something or maybe cooler than I thought and understood.

After a while, I stopped hanging out with Nathan and the rest of the Jewish clicker kids. They were fun, but I started being drawn to a more respectable group – the burnouts. The burnouts were doing everything the Jews weren't – cutting out of school, smoking weed and drinking.

Nathan and those guys didn't do that shit. They were good students. They were fun guys but didn't do drugs, they didn't drink, they didn't cut out of school. They were those strange types of high school students who actually went to school.

Weird.

CHAPTER 4

PRANK HIGH

Without Nathan I kept doing pranks, but mostly by myself and for my own amusement.

The cops were my frequent targets. I got a lot of excitement and a rush when I would fuck with cops. Because I felt wronged and emotionally wounded by my cop dad, pranks made me feel strong and vindicated.

Sometimes I'd anonymously call the cops on myself from a payphone. I'd say something like, "This guy was involved in a robbery," and describe my car and license plate. Then I would listen to my police scanner until they pulled me over. I liked the fact that the cops were following me. It was a weird fucking thrill game I played. I knew I wouldn't get in trouble. Even negative attention from cops somehow gave me inner satisfaction.

When I was bored, I'd go across the street from Brill's Supermarket near where I lived and call 911 from a payphone. I'd tell the emergency operator in a panicked voice there was a holdup happening at Brill's, and that I just escaped the gunmen through the back door. Then I hung up before they could ask more questions.

I'd move well away from the phone booth and watch the drama unfold. Cops would roll up from every direction and get out with their guns drawn. Then they stormed into Brill's Supermarket. I'm sure they scared the shit out of customers and employees who were just going about their daily business. Of course the cops would come back out after a minute giving the all-clear sign.

One time while I was doing this prank, I got more than I expected when a police helicopter showed up and hovered just a hundred feet over the store, shaking the whole neighborhood. This was much better than anything on TV.

My new burnout friends were also into pulling pranks. We drove around at night playing mailbox baseball, knocking them off with bats. Drove up on people's lawns doing neutral drops, tearing up their front yards. Knocking over garbage pails, throwing deck furniture into pools. Egging cars and houses on Halloween. Respectable citizens each and every one of us.

There was a park where the cops patrolled at night trying to catch kids hanging out and drinking and such. But the park wasn't accessible to cars, so the cops had to go in on foot. When they left, my friends and I would rub dog shit all over their fucking cars, spit on it then top it with ice cream. We'd go sit a few houses away on the front lawn. The cops knew we did it and would come talk to us. But they couldn't prove anything.

Even when they did catch us doing stuff, because my father was a cop, the police would usually just tell us to get the fuck out of there. My older brother Vinnie was wild. He would pull down his pants, moon the cops and tell them to kiss his ass. I'm sure it was humiliating for my father. But to us it was fun and exciting.

I also brought my pranks to high school. I wasn't bringing homework or sports trophies to Plainedge High, so I contributed in a different way.

One day during class I got a pass to the bathroom. But instead of going to the bathroom, I went to an empty locker in the hall and put a blockbuster firework in the top part. A blockbuster is a quarter stick of dynamite. I lit a Marlboro cigarette, poked a hole into the filter and inserted the fuse. The cigarette started burning down slowly. I hurried back to class and waited all eager and ready to get out of school and cause some excitement.

After what seemed like forever, I heard a loud explosion followed by the ringing of the fire bell. The whole school filed out. The fire department came, along with the police and bomb squad with bomb-sniffing dogs.

I met up with some friends and we left school grounds to smoke some cigarettes and goof off. I didn't tell any of them it was me who did the explosion. After an hour, we came back to school and everyone was still outside waiting for the all-clear to go back in.

Doing that kind of prank made me feel like I had power and influence over all these people. I also found the whole thing funny, amusing and thrilling.

Cut to the tenth grade. I was in biology – my most hated class. Then suddenly the fire bell rang and the whole school was told to leave the building. It was the middle of winter and freezing out. Almost none of us had our jackets because they rushed us out of the building so fast and didn't let us go to our lockers. Standing outside we saw the fire department, police and dogs arrive. Word spread that it was a bomb scare, so it seemed we would be outside for a while as they searched the entire school.

This was definitely not my doing.

After a good while, they told us to go back inside to class. But I decided to skip Spanish and go to the cafeteria to get a bagel and juice instead.

But it turns out when you have class, they want you to be in there instead of having brunch by yourself. This teacher Mr. Sherman stormed into the cafeteria and shouted, "Hey Bootsolino! What are you doing here? Come here."

Being the rebel I'd been the last couple of years, I didn't listen to him and ran out into the hallway with Mr. Sherman in pursuit behind. I turned a corner and saw the chairman of the social studies department, Dr. Petrakis, and a female student walking towards me. Dr. P would often come into our history class and tell us cool Greek myths. I slowed down to a fast walk so it wouldn't look like I was running away and in trouble. Once I passed them, I began running again.

Just then, Dr. Petrakis froze and fell forward without even bending his knees or bracing his fall. He landed face first onto the hard marble floor. The girl walking with him screamed hysterically. We were the only three people in the hall.

I approached Dr. Petrakis and rolled him over onto his back. Mr. Sherman turned the corner and saw that Dr. P needed help. He stopped in his tracks and ran to the nurse's office. The first thing I noticed was a large gash on Dr. Petrakis' forehead. And he was bleeding heavily.

I took off my T-shirt and used it to apply direct pressure to his wound. I recently learned first aid in health class and that was one of the courses where I actually paid attention. His eyes were wide open and darting back and forth as if he was in shock but couldn't speak. I could tell he was scared. His chest started to rise, so I loosened his tie and ripped his shirt open, sending buttons flying.

I unfastened his belt and undid his pants so as not to constrict his breathing and whatever was happening with his chest. Then I checked for breathing and there was none. I tilted his head back and began to perform mouth-to-mouth. I formed a tight seal around his mouth with mine, pinched his nose and filled his lungs with air... to no avail.

It was at this point that Dr. Petrakis threw up directly into my mouth. I gagged and spit out the vomit then used my fingers to clear his mouth and throat. I did this and he was able to get in a few good breaths just as the nurse and gym teacher showed up. They told me to step aside while they began mouth-to-mouth and CPR.

As I took one last look at Dr. Petrakis, he gave me a look that one does when they're saying, "I don't want to die... I have so much more to do in life... I love my wife and children and will miss them and can't say goodbye... no no no I don't want to die... please don't let me die!" I was shaken and shirtless with blood on my chest and hands.

The county police and ambulance crew arrived and took over. The first thing they did was fumble around with this breathing apparatus that had two facemasks and a connecting tube. You were to tightly seal one over your face and put the other mask over the patient's face. This was their more hygienic way of performing mouth-to-mouth without having to touch Dr. Petrakis directly.

But the paramedics couldn't get a tight seal and were fumbling with the piece of shit device. Even though they were sworn lifesavers, they were scared of doing mouth-to-mouth and catching something from a 70-year-old man. I was really pissed.

They escorted me down to the nurse's office. Over the school loud speaker, everyone was instructed to remain in their classrooms even though the period was over. I sat in the nurse's office and tried to calm down and process what just happened.

Mr. Sherman, who'd previously been chasing me, came into the nurse's office and said, "At first I thought you knocked Dr. Petrakis over when you ran around the corner, but the girl who was with him told me that wasn't so. And I just wanted to apologize for thinking that. Thank you for what you did."

Wow, I was thinking. I was just about to get in trouble and now he was apologizing to me? The nurse came back to her office and I recounted to her and the gym teacher what happened. They were impressed by my quick thinking and that I used what I learned in health class.

From the window, we saw Dr. Petrakis being loaded into the ambulance and taken to the hospital about a half-mile away. The nurse asked if I felt like going home for the day. But I thought of the reaction from Mr. Sherman and thought, "No, I don't want to go home. I'd rather stay and garner more of this positive attention from all the teachers," most of whom considered me a problem student with truancy and behavioral issues.

My mom came to school, brought me a clean T-shirt and I returned halfway through math class. When I entered the classroom, everyone looked at me as if they all wanted to say something, but didn't know what. Word had spread of my "heroics." So I sat down and basked in a hero's glow.

Not five minutes later, the principal came on the loudspeaker and sadly announced that Dr. Petrakis just died at the hospital.

Everyone in the class looked at me. I was in shock, and tears rolled down my face. I kept thinking of his eyes looking into mine and silently pleading not to let him die. Dr. Petrakis didn't die at the hospital. He died there on the floor as those EMTs fumbled with that mouth-to-mouth contraption, and I blamed them.

Now this was 1983 and the school didn't offer counselors to anyone affected by this, so I just dealt with it on my own. That afternoon, I went over to my good friend Ron's house to tell him about everything that happened. He hadn't been in school that day.

Ron's mom answered the door. She was wearing a one-piece housecoat typical of Italian women from Brooklyn, where she was from.

Ron's dad was in the den sitting on his recliner, drinking scotch and smoking a cigar. The only thing I ever saw Ron's dad do was sit in that chair, drink and smoke. Ron said his dad suffered from alcoholic blackouts. At night, he would wander the house and think the dining room was the bathroom. He would piss and shit in the dining room drawers then go back to sleep. I don't think they hosted too many dinner parties.

Ron had Black Sabbath posters hanging all over his room and pot plants growing in the closet. His room always had a thick cloud of Marlboro smoke. Since I had such protective parents, I thought he was the coolest guy. His parents even let him put a lock on his bedroom door! He had no rules.

We sat on his bed and smoked Marlboros. Then we hung our heads out the window and called to his pet duck Charley outside in a pen. Ron occasionally fed Charley some of his Valium pills. I said hello to the duck then we shut the window. It was freezing out.

I asked Ron why he wasn't in school that day. He said he just didn't feel like going and instead wanted to stay home and pull a prank. His parents didn't care either way.

Earlier that morning, Ron wrote up a short manifesto for a group he created called OTFUTS - ORGANIZATION TO FUCK UP THE SYSTEM. He stayed home all day, except when he went to the payphone at the nearby shopping center. Ron called our school and made his voice sound real deep and serious. He read his OTFUTS manifesto to the school secretary and added, "We have planted multiple explosive devices in the school. This is not a joke."

Ron told me about this prank, laughed hysterically and asked about the reactions at school.

Now I'm all for fucking around and for a bit of anarchy. But what Ron didn't realize was how this prank impacted that day. During the bomb threat caused by his call, the whole school stood outside in the freezing cold for over an hour. Not long after coming back in, Dr. Petrakis suffered a stroke and died. To me, it didn't take a rocket scientist to conclude that being outside in the cold and the stress from that more than likely triggered the stroke that killed him.

When I laid this out to Ron, he got real scared. Scared that he killed someone with a prank, scared he would get caught, scared he would go to jail, scared that he would go to hell even though he never went to church or seemed to practice the Catholic religion he was baptized in.

Ron was my good friend and I was directly involved in this because the man practically died in my arms. I thought to myself how easily I could have been in the same position given my own recent foolish pranks. I felt just as guilty and told him neither of us would ever tell another soul what he did that morning. And it was a pact that we made and I kept until now that I'm sharing this.

Over the years, Ron expressed how truly guilty he felt and couldn't come to terms with it. He said a few times how he deserved to die. I would tell him he could do penance by making his life a silent devotion to Dr. Petrakis and do good things in his name while living an honorable life. Only Ron and God needed to know his penance. He would agree but I could tell he always doubted this.

Ron's life was plagued with drug abuse and some overdoses. A few years later, he dropped a plugged-in toaster into the bathtub, killing himself. He was never the same after the bomb scare, and I've carried it with me until now and remain haunted by it.

* * *

You might think this incident would scare me straight and steer me away from a life of pulling pranks. But I never really stopped.

The big difference was that now I would only try to fuck with people who slighted me, not random innocent civilians. At least a dozen times, I would have a run-in with someone or have words with them or just generally felt punked by them. But I was too soft and scared to fight and not confident enough to challenge them directly. But I had to get revenge and feel like I did something.

Dante Ricapito was a weed dealer who lived in my neighborhood. He was 21 and I was 15. I once gave him $60 to buy an ounce of weed. But the guy stiffed me, saying he ran out of weed but would keep all my money anyway.

"Fuck off and go tell your father," Dante said as he cackled and mocked me, knowing my father was a cop and would kick my ass if he knew I had anything to do with pot. I knew immediately that I had to get back at Dante and get him good.

So I went into the woods behind my house and planted a handful of marijuana seeds deep in the brush. Every few days I'd bring jugs of water and make sure they were watered well. By early September, I had around fifteen plants growing in my backyard, each about a half-foot high. I dug up all the weed plants - roots and all - and snuck into Dante's backyard. I planted the pot in his yard hidden amongst the dense bushes and foliage.

The next day, I called the local police precinct and asked to speak with the narcotics detectives. They transferred me.

"Detective Stewart."

In a voice that had grown deep for my age, I said, "Yes, I need to talk to you, but wish to remain anonymous, as this has to do with my son and I'm handling him on this end. But I want to inform you of a serious problem we have in my neighborhood."

This piqued the detective's interest and he assured that I didn't have to reveal my name.

I said, "Well I recently found my son with a large bag of marijuana in his room. My son and I have always had an honest relationship so I asked where he got it from, and he told me it was Dante Ricapito, who lives on Euclid Avenue."

The detective wrote all this down. I went on and said, "My son informed me that this guy Dante supplies all the kids in the neighborhood with weed."

Detective Stewart asked if I would allow my son to make a drug purchase from Dante that they could monitor. Then they would have the evidence needed to make a quick arrest and put this guy out of business. I told him no, I wouldn't want my son involved in that, but had something just as helpful.

"My son told me Dante grows weed in his backyard and has several plants growing there."

The detective said he would "take care of this parasite." I laid it on thick, acting all upset that this guy was poisoning our youth and I hoped this wouldn't be brushed aside because it was a big case. Detective Stewart gave his assurance that he would personally head the investigation.

The next morning, there were 8 marked and unmarked cop cars along with the local news media in front of Dante's house. It turned out that in addition to weed, the guido piece of shit had a triple beam scale and an ounce of coke in his room. The dummy was selling coke on the side. I didn't even know about this but that was an extra bonus. Dante's face, name, house and address were all in the local news. And it was an arrest he had to pay a nice chunk of change to get a lawyer for, because he wasn't poor enough for a public defender.

This is the type of vengeance I took on a number of people over the years. My motto was you better not fuck with me. I will fuck you up worse than an ass beating would. It made me feel superior.

* * *

After my heroics trying to save Dr. Petrakis at school, I felt like I bought a little time and could do what I wanted and not be bothered by teachers or administration. And for a while, the school did let me slide on my truancy and behavior issues.

But it just continued, and I showed up less and less and started getting in trouble again. I had terrible grades. And it wasn't because I was stupid. I just didn't apply myself and never thought about my life and future. I didn't have any idea what I wanted to do, and no one ever tried to get me to think about it.

I just wanted people to accept me and be my friend. I was a lost soul.

So the second month of 11th grade I just said fuck it and dropped out of high school. I signed myself out, and the school had no objections. I was 15 years old and that was the biggest mistake of my life, because my life got so screwed up after that. I just said fuck it.

I also told my parents I was leaving home. They had no objections either.

CHAPTER 5

GIMME THE LOOT

By the age of fifteen, I just hated living at home. There was constant fighting with my parents. My truancy from school and complete disinterest in subjects. Rebellious behavior, run-ins with the cops. And my father finding pot in my room. Lots of fun nights at the Bootsolino residence.

I finally told my parents I was leaving. And their reply was, "Good, and if you do leave, don't ever think of coming back."

So I left. And my parents never searched the neighborhood looking for me like I secretly wished they would, so I could have a warm meal and sleep in my bed. Soon my friend Sean and my older brother Vinnie joined me.

We had no money, no jobs and no homes. We subsisted by crashing at our friends' houses and eating meals there. At night we stole change from unlocked cars on the street and shopping center parking lots. In one car we found a nice big tent. We took it and started spending our nights camping in the woods by Massapequa Creek.

Come Thanksgiving Day, we started missing those turkey dinners with our families. We were at our friend Ron's house and thought maybe we could at least go buy some turkey sandwiches and have our own version of a nice family holiday.

Then it hit me - Why don't we do some burglaries around dinnertime? A lot of families would be out late having dinner with their relatives.

My brother Vinnie didn't want any part of home burglaries, concerned we would get caught and in real trouble. Vinnie decided to go have dinner at our actual house. I don't know how much begging he had to do, but my parents let him back in. As for me, I wasn't ready to give up yet. Now it was just Sean and me. I was 15 and he was 16.

Sean said the burglaries sounded like a good idea. Ron gave us a crowbar and flashlight. As it got dark, Sean and I walked a few blocks and found a street where the houses were obscured by hedges and surrounded by short fences.

The first house was dark and no cars were in the driveway. It looked empty, but I went up and rang the doorbell anyway. Should someone answer, I would ask for a fictitious name and play it off like I must have the wrong house for

Thanksgiving dinner. That was before GPS, when these kinds of interactions were much more common.

But when I rang the bell there was no answer.

Let's do it now or chicken out!

My knees were shaking. I was so fucking nervous but made my way around the back. I called out to Sean, who hopped the fence and joined me.

Entry seemed simple. All these houses had basements with small windows. I just sat my ass in front of the window and kicked and pushed against the latch to break it. I slithered into the basement feet-first and landed on a washing machine before making it to the floor.

On went the flashlight. Sean followed. We found the stairs leading up, opened the basement door to the main floor and there we were - in some stranger's house uninvited, ready to rob them of their things and sense of security they felt living there.

I hit the master bedroom and told Sean to stay by the window as a lookout. I made sure to cup the flashlight and hide the light emitting so neighbors couldn't see.

I opened the dresser drawers and grabbed a bunch of chains, rings and watches. On top of the dresser I spotted a ring with a big diamond in it. Score. I then took some cash and jewelry from other rooms.

Before leaving I went into the bathroom and checked the medicine cabinet, looking for drugs I could recognize. I looked for any prescription medicine bottles labeled FOR PAIN or DON'T TAKE WITH ALCOHOL. I spotted a bottle of Valiums and quickly grabbed them. My winter jacket pockets were filled with booty from the house.

Feeling we were done and still being scared shitless, we exited the house through the back door and quickly climbed over the back fence to the main road. I gave Sean a breakdown of what we scored.

Despite still being a bit shaken, I now had a certain degree of fearlessness and didn't want to stop. I told Sean it didn't look like the next door neighbors were home either, so why not hit that house too, cause it should be just as easy as the first. When I said all he had to do was be the lookout by the window again, he quickly agreed.

So we went through the same routine. Rang the bell, no answer, went around back, pushed in the window, slithered down inside and made our way up to the main floor.

Again I went right for the master bedroom, taking all the jewelry I could find, not knowing if it was good or bad or just plain costume junk. This time I also found plastic tubes filled with silver half dollars. There must have been 20 of those tubes.

Now I couldn't fit all this in my pockets so I found a gym bag in the bedroom closet, which I loaded all the loot into. I also found a box with old baseball cards and grabbed them as well.

I hit the other rooms and took a camera and a few pieces of jewelry. Even grabbed the contents of a piggy bank. Again I hit the medicine cabinet but didn't see anything good.

As I went to tell Sean we should get going, something caught my eye. I spied in the living room a cabinet full of Hummel Figurines. My mom collected these dolls and would often say they were worth a lot of money. Thanks mom. I got another bag and some newspaper from the kitchen, quickly wrapped up about 15 of these Hummels and put them in the bag.

Again we went out the rear door, and again I said to Sean that the next house looked empty as well. So why not hit it then call it quits for the night? Sean readily agreed.

We stashed the loot in bushes by the fence next to the road. Again we went through the same routine, which by now we had down to a science. We were in and out of the house in under ten minutes, scoring more jewelry, cash, and even a 6-pack of beer that we drank on our train ride into the city.

On the Long Island Railroad, we took a closer look at the stolen booty. We looked for 14k tags on the jewelry. Some had it, some didn't. Because it was the Thanksgiving holiday, all of the places to fence this stuff were closed that night. So we took some of the stolen cash and used it to get a room at the YMCA in Manhattan. In our room we separated the booty into different categories and waited for morning.

The next day, not knowing where to fence the stolen loot, we just walked around Midtown West. The first place we went was a jewelry store on 8th Avenue near the Port Authority train station. We went in there and spoke to the Korean owner. Now I was chancing it, because this guy could just call the cops, but it's a chance I took.

There was a large plexiglass wall between us and the Korean owner. I doubt the partition was actually bullet-proof, but there was a sign saying it was. There was a small window to pass things through. I just took a bunch of shit from my pocket and passed it through to him. He looked at the loot, then looked at me, then looked around to see if anyone was watching. And then he went to work testing the gold, weighing and checking a couple of diamonds.

"1200 dollars."

I said, "That's it?"

He said yes and that was a good price. I said okay, but I would be back with more and wanted him to do me right. He said that he always would. He didn't ask for ID or log my name as was required by law. Just passed me $1,200 cash. I was elated to have that much money so quick in my pocket.

Now I had the costume jewelry shit to try and sell. After an hour or so of looking around, I found a small store on 9th Avenue in Hell's Kitchen run by a real fat Jewish guy. This guy bought all my costume jewelry and told me he would always take whatever I had. He didn't ask for ID either, and just paid me a few hundred bucks.

I left to try and find a place to sell the Hummels. This took some searching but I finally found a place on 5th Avenue that bought all the dolls. And I'm sure the guy ripped me off, but again I got a few hundred no questions asked.

Now it was time to unload the silver half dollars. I spotted a large coin store on 5th Avenue. I was buzzed in and made my way to the rear of the store, where an old guy looked me up and down and said, "Whatcha got for me, kid?"

I gleefully pulled out my treasure from the bag and placed it in front of him. He counted the coins, punched the keys on his calculator and said he'd give me $800. Deal.

One thing I learned that day was how many seemingly honest businessmen were criminals like me. No, they didn't actually go and steal but they played a big role by profiting and participating.

Altogether Sean and I had around $2,800. For two kids in the early 1980s, it was a fortune. I let him keep the baseball cards since he collected them.

Thinking we shouldn't head back to Long Island while our burglaries were being investigated, Sean and I bought bus tickets to visit his cousins outside Baltimore. Down there we met girls who said our New York accents made us sound sexy, cool and dangerous. And we did feel kind of cool and dangerous.

While in Baltimore, Sean's cousins got him on the phone with his parents, who tried convincing him to go live at home when he went back to New York. And he did just that. I really didn't know how fucked up his home life was or even why he left. His mom knew my mom from church and she always seemed nice. His dad was in a wheelchair from an accident while working on a garbage truck.

Sean's older brother Dwight lived in their basement. We'd often see him walking back and forth from 7-Eleven with shopping bags full of beer. Some years later, Dwight blew his brains out with a shotgun. And Sean had to clean up the mess.

Now I was really on my own. But with the money from stealing, I was able to rent my own apartment – a major upgrade from the tent. I always had cash and weed since I continued to do burglaries on a regular basis.

CHAPTER 6

THE GAY TEEN SEX CHAPTER

I took a break from burglaries for a few weeks and just hung out with my friend Pete and a bunch of 15-16 year old girls we met at the mall.

The girls loved to get high, fuck and give blowjobs. Pete and I fucked them all. At times in my apartment – which had two large beds on either side - we'd each be fucking a girl then say "switch" and swap girls. We had the girls eating each other out and two at once sucking our cocks while the other guy watched or fucked one of the girls from behind. None of us seemed to have any sexual hang-ups.

It was also at this time that I started going to local gay cruise spots on Long Island. I don't know where the urge came from, but damn I had it.

Parking lots, gay clubs, park bathrooms and porno shops with video booths. Back then there was no internet, Grindr,

Scruff or anything like gay guys have today. Finding guys meant actually having to go outside.

I would be at rest stops and meet up with guys in their 40s and 50s. I let these older guys suck my cock and I'd nut in their mouths. This was mostly what my gay experiences consisted of. I liked the excitement of hooking up and doing it where there was a danger of getting caught.

But I did this all in secret. Nobody had any idea. And I was in constant fear that someone would see me doing gay stuff and tell everyone. Then I'd just have to kill myself cause I wouldn't be able to live with people knowing that I liked men.

So I secretly started hitting the gay clubs. My usual M.O. was to eye up a cute twink. A twink is a young skinny effeminate gay guy. I'd approach the twink, make out with him a bit and then suggest we go to my car. I would have him suck my dick. Then I'd leave and drive home satisfied. Every now and then if I found the guy to be real cute, and he just wanted me to come over to sleep with him with no fucking and such, I would take them up on it then leave before they woke up in the morning.

I stayed at the YMCA in the city a few times. It was the early 1980s and real cruisy and gay. I was 15 and pedophile bait. Dude, I could just walk into a guy's room and see how they were looking and acting. I could tell the cruisy situations. There wasn't any kind of security or regulations.

Everything was pretty blatant. I would hook up with a guy or two or three a night there. I wouldn't let them fuck me because I hadn't been fucked yet. Just letting guys blow me but I wouldn't blow them. They could jerk off on me and jerk off in my face. I liked that.

Another thing I'd do was go into porno booth places and watch gay sex movies. You'd walk past these little porno-viewing booths, and guys would open the curtain and be sitting there with their pants open. They'd look at you and say come on in. If they looked decent and sane, I'd go into their booth and we'd jerk off together or the guy would blow me. That was my big thing – getting guys to blow me.

One day, I went down to a gay porn store that a guy at the YMCA told me about. For $10 you could go downstairs to a room and find yourself in what could best be described as a gay sex dungeon.

Downstairs there were naked guys trying to entice other guys to follow them. In another part of the basement was a circle jerk with about 15-20 guys. Different corners had guys blowing each other and some fucking. I started watching two guys in their early 20s who were fucking and I took out my cock and jerked off watching them.

This was a new experience for me.

It didn't take long before a not-so-ugly guy came over and dropped to his knees in front of me. The guy just started sucking. Within thirty seconds I blew a massive load in his mouth.

I walked to another part of the basement where some twink was getting bukake'd on by about 8-10 guys. I found this to be a big turn on and even though I had just came, I got very hard again and joined in. While I was jerking off to spray this guy down, I secretly wanted it to be me getting hit with all that cum.

But I did my part and when I was about to nut, I positioned myself right in front of his face where he knelt with his mouth open invitingly, hoping to catch my load. I coated his face then took my fingers and rubbed the cum into and around his face, ending with a nice wad on my fingers feeding it to his awaiting and appreciative mouth!

* * *

Also at that age, I began to combine my appetite for gay sex with my tendency to rob people. I would sit by the Port Authority exit near 8th Avenue. Within minutes, I would see an older guy slowing down and checking me out. They would pass a few times and I'd lock eyes and smile. They'd approach and ask how I was doing and did I want to take a walk.

It didn't take long for them to offer $20 to suck me off in the Port Authority parking garage stairwell. I told them sure that sounded great. So we'd go into the stairwell and I'd pull my cock out and have him start sucking it. Sometimes

I'd finish, and sometimes I wouldn't. But then I'd pull out a knife on him. And they'd be so scared man.

And I'd be like, "Motherfucker just give me your fucking money. Give it all to me now. If you know what's better for you, you ain't gonna say shit. Cause I'll tell the fucking cops that you just sucked off a fucking 15-year-old. Give me your fucking money now."

And they'd give me the money. I did this 12-15 times and even turned my straight friend Pete onto it. Pete was real cute and young looking but also very straight. He'd tell me that yes he'd let the ugly freaks suck his cock, but it was all about the money.

Cut to Pete and me riding the Long Island Railroad back home late one night. We'd spent the whole day hustling guys in the city and both of us had tons of cash in our pockets. I told Pete how I'd like to suck him off sometime. At first he laughed. Then after a few moments, Pete said, "How about right now?"

We looked around. There were two other people in our train car, but they were all the way on the other end facing the opposite direction. So Pete pulled it out and, oh man, it was beautiful. Had to be a nice thick 7-8 inches. I went down on him right there in the train seat of the LIRR. Then I jerked him off and had him shoot it in my face. God I love that!

Then my "straight" buddy Pete said he wanted to fuck me. I'd never been fucked before, but figured if there was ever a good time to try, it was right now with Pete.

I couldn't see us doing it in the train seat. So I looked around for ideas, then suggested the train bathroom. We went in the bathroom. I dropped my pants and underwear to my ankles and bent over, grabbing the toilet as the train rumbled and jolted along. He played with his cock to get it fully erect and spit a few times on my pig ass, and then ever so slowly started probing and inserting his beautiful cock inside me. I couldn't believe he was in me and I was so fucking happy. He started pumping slowly then picked up speed.

He must have went on for almost 15 minutes before exploding in my ass. He was calling me his girl and saying how good of a bitch I was and how tight my pussy was. This turned me on!

*   *   *

One night I met this guy at Port Authority, thinking I would have him suck me off then rob him like I'd done so many times before. But then as we were walking he suggested we go up to his apartment nearby, smoke some weed, drink and hang out. I sized him up and saw he wasn't bad looking and seemed like a normal guy. Slightly dweeby and harmless, kind of looked like Egon from *Ghostbusters*. So I said okay. I thought maybe I'll rob him, maybe I won't.

Dude, as soon as we got into his apartment he wound up doing this fucken chokehold on me, like a karate move, and pulled a switchblade on me. He said, "Pull down your pants, lie down on your stomach on the bed." And he raped me.

He had a knife to my neck the whole time. I thought I was gonna die dude. I thought my mother was gonna find out and this was the fucked up way I was gonna die. The guy was telling me shit like, "You fuck around and I'm gonna kill you and throw you out the window like I've done before to other guys. People will think your faggot ass killed yourself!" I was like this guy's a fucking psycho.

Dude, after it was done he got all nice and thanked me. He asked if I wanted to get dinner with him and his friends. I was like no I gotta go.

I couldn't report it because I was a 15-year-old runaway. I would have had to go back home to my parents. I was a fucking burglar. I didn't want anyone to know I was gay, and I didn't want anyone to know I was raped. It was all fucking guilt and shame.

After that, I retired from my career as a hustler-mugger.

* * *

When it came to girls I tried to be straight, hoping my gay feelings would go away. I often got freaky and kinky with girls to overcompensate. 2 girls and me, me and a buddy running a train on her, doing a girl at the same time, swapping partners during motel orgies where up to 8-10 couples were going at it. I got into being tied up. Lots of anal with chicks and had chicks finger my ass and eat it.

Having a boyfriend wasn't even a thought dude. No one in my life knew shit about me. It was all about sex. I could have a regular hookup but never anything serious.

This was my existence. Lots of hot sex but nobody to love, and no one to love me.

CHAPTER 7

CAUGHT UP

Getting back to the burglaries, I was still doing a few home robberies a week. I always had a drawer full of cash in my apartment and a large wad with at least a thousand in my left pocket.

Now and then Sean joined me for a burglary or two, but for the most part it was a one-man crime wave. Word was spreading about a burglar who broke into houses with similar patterns and targets.

Every so often, I'd think about the people I took things from. My mother told me how before they moved to Long Island their house in Queens was burglarized. Her mother's wedding ring was stolen. She said how she couldn't even live in that house anymore, how the sanctity of their home felt violated.

And here I was doing that to other people. I always thought of that. But I'd dismiss it quickly cause I was able to. I was a cold kind of son of a bitch. Selfish and heartless.

This one night in Manhattan, I was on 8th Avenue and 44th street when a not-so-bad-looking black chick approached me. She started flirting saying, "Hey, you're a handsome motherfucker. How 'bout you let me suck your dick."

An offer like this doesn't come a guy's way every day. I said, "Fuck yeah. Where should we do this?"

She said, "Right here in the doorway baby." I looked around quickly and said what the fuck. So I unzipped my pants and pulled out my raging hard-on.

"What a nice cock," she said and started sucking. She paused for a moment. "Keep a lookout for the cops." I agreed and scanned the area for police while she got back to work. People were walking by on the sidewalk and I saw one guy notice us, but he kept walking because hey it was NYC and Times Square before it got nice.

Soon I nutted in her mouth and said thanks as I tucked my cock back into my pants. "Anytime baby," she said and went on her way.

In the afterglow of this romantic encounter, I was feeling hungry and decided to get a slice of pizza. I reached into my pocket for some cash, and fuck me! She got me. That black chick stole all the cash from my pants pocket while blowing me. Then telling me to keep a lookout for cops was a further distraction. I'd been conned and robbed. I felt like a fucking idiot and was pissed because I just got took for about $1,500 cash. I went around looking for her, but she was gone.

The next day I was still pissed at myself for being so stupid. I tried making up for the lost cash by doing a couple more burglaries than usual. I was in this house robbing it the routine way. Rang the doorbell, no response, kicked the basement window in, searched the house, got the booty. A tisket a tasket.

I made my way to the main floor of the house. All the shades were closed, and from the smell I could tell elderly people lived there. I went to the bedroom and the pickings were slim. I took what was there and shoved it into my pocket. Went for the medicine cabinet and there were lots of script bottles, but I didn't recognize any of the names so I left them. The house was a bust. Had to find a better one.

Just then, something caught my eye in the living room near the couch. It was a person.

Oh fuck!

I got closer, and saw that there was an old man on the floor.

I went over and carefully checked to see if he was bleeding and if there was a heartbeat. He did have a beat and a pulse, though it seemed really weak.

Then I went back into this old man's bedroom, emptied my pockets of what I'd stolen and returned all the loot to where I found it. I went into the kitchen and called an ambulance. I told the dispatcher about the guy and said the door would be unlocked. I exited through the front door, leaving it open for emergency workers.

I always knew that inside of me there was someone good and caring, but that he rarely showed up. Here I was a drug user, dealer and thief. But whenever I did a kind act, I felt so special and good inside. I always wanted to hold on to that feeling. Ever since I was a little boy, I felt that was why I was put on this earth – to help others. I'd tell myself I was doing these bad things so that some day I would be able to help others and do good things.

*   *   *

It was a weekday. I picked out three houses in a row on Lakeshore Boulevard to burgle. They all had hedges good for coverage and were nicely maintained houses, hence there must be some goodies inside. I didn't see any alarm company signs or stickers on their front doors.

I knocked on the first house's door. No answer. I was in and out in ten minutes. Then went on to the second house. Same routine.

But as I was finishing up inside the third house, I peeked outside the living room window and noticed some unusual activity outside. Evidently, the occupant of the second house I burglarized had just come home to find it ransacked and called the cops. One marked police car arrived and parked in front of the house.

I immediately fucking panicked and knew I needed to get the fuck out of there. I opened the rear door to escape over the backyard fence. As I opened the door, a loud police siren sounded. Fuck fuck fuck!

Panic. Fleeing. Fleeing. Get away at all costs.

I darted through the yard and over the fence into the rear neighbor's yard. The cop out front saw me and gunned his engine to catch up. I ran down the street as a jogger was coming the other way. Turned out the jogger was an off-duty cop, who joined in on the chase.

I made it out to a large boulevard and cop cars were coming from every direction. I dodged them left and right and ran behind some stores, where I ditched my loot bag in the back of a truck. I ran into a swamp and crouched between the swamp and some small pine trees. Two cops ran in and were standing just a couple feet from me. I stayed still and quiet and listened to their conversation. The cops said I must have gone over the fence to the adjacent area. They also mentioned that I ditched my loot bag in back of the truck.

I should have stayed put, but instead went right where I heard the cops say I would probably go. Stupid! I hopped the fence and made it around the front of someone's house and hid in the bushes. I peeked through the bushes and saw cop cars scouring the neighborhood.

Just then, Johnny Good Citizen came out on his front porch, pointed towards me and shouted at the cops.

"Here he is! He's hiding here."

The officers converged and approached the bushes with weapons drawn. I raised my hands and gave up. I remember saying to myself, "It's all over Joey." Life, future, prospects. Done.

I got cuffed and thrown in the back of one of the dozens of cop cars.

"What's your name?" asked a cop.

"Joe."

"Joe what?"

"Joe Bootsolino."

"Joe Bootsolino? Are you Vincent Bootsolino's son?"

I shamefully looked down and said yes.

The cop smacked me real hard across the face and called me a dumb motherfucker. I knew I deserved that. As a cop's son, I disgraced my father and myself.

They took me to the station and started the interrogation. The cops said that they already picked up my brother Vinnie and he told them everything, so I might as well tell them too. They said they knew my brother helped with some of these burglaries. I said to myself that Vinnie never did a burglary and these guys were just fishing for me to sell him out.

I looked at the cops, snickered and said I didn't know what the fuck they were talking about. They said they knew I committed other burglaries and witnesses said there was another guy. But I never sold out Sean.

I was arraigned the next morning and charged with 4 counts of burglary. It eventually became 5 counts because I got busted from my fingerprints being found in another house. I made the news for the crimes themselves, and for being the first suspect caught using a new computerized program that linked fingerprints on file with those found at crime scenes.

The papers called me the "Stuff Your Pocket Burglar."

CHAPTER 8

JAIL TALES

Bail was set at $10,000. While my family got the money together, I was taken to the Nassau County jail and put in the youth tier for criminals age 16-21. From what I'd heard about this place, it was a place to fear.

I knew a couple of the correctional officers, as they were neighbors of my parents. On my first night, the COs called me out and gave me a carton of Marlboros my mom sent. They said to open the carton before I went back to the tier and hide the packs in the waistband of my jumpsuit.

The next day my lawyer came for our first meeting. Before going down, I took the cigs in my one-man cell and hid them under the far end of the mattress. When I got back, they were gone. Someone stole my cigarettes. But what the fuck was I gonna do - fight the whole tier? For the next couple days, the black guys who usually smoked Newports were all smoking Marlboros. But what the fuck was I gonna do?

After ten days, I got bailed out and stayed with a Catholic priest who ran a group home for troubled teens. I stayed there for almost a year while my case went through its stages. As my sentencing date got closer, and it looked like I was gonna get at least 18 months upstate, I began to panic about the whole situation. So I swallowed an entire bottle of Librium. I wasn't thinking right, was scared to death of prison and tried to kill myself.

I was rushed to the hospital in an ambulance and they poured that charcoal shit down my throat. They admitted me to a children's psych ward. While there, I met a real sexual crazy girl named Tess who loved to give me blowjobs.

After a couple weeks in the psych hospital, they took me to the courthouse for sentencing. I was gonna be sentenced for 5 burglaries. They knew I probably committed dozens more, but they just wanted to complete the case and get me out of there.

The judge gave me four to six months in prison and granted youthful offender status. That meant I would have no record after completing my time. I would not only be going back to the Gladiator Academy for a short stint. I'd then be shipped upstate to a prison, which frightened the shit out of me. This was Groveland Prison in the 1980s.

Most of the time though, upstate wasn't crazy like the stories I heard or what you see in movies. Even worse, it was mostly just extremely boring and went very slowly. I wrote letters to family and friends. The slutty girl Tess from the psych ward wrote me the kinkiest letters, which served their masturbatory purpose.

I had two fights in prison, though one wasn't really a fight. I was housed in a dorm and there was this huge muscular black guy from Buffalo named Jaymore. He was walking past my bunk towards his. I don't know what I said, but Jaymore lunged at me with a closed fist and punched me so fucking hard across my right eye I could immediately feel it swell up.

I knew I was supposed to go after him. But fuck that cause he could kill me. The COs saw my swelled eye and asked what happened. I said that I fell. They sent me to the prison nurse, who couldn't do much but did take notice of my depression, which was hard to hide. The medium security prison didn't have a psych ward, so they sent me 45 minutes away to Attica State Prison. Now I'd heard something of this place and it sure put the fear of God into me. Driving up there was a scary experience.

I was escorted up to the psych ward for 72 hours of observation. While there, a guy sitting next to me saw my bruised eye and said, "What the fuck happened to you?"

I said, "Nothing. Just a fall."

When I turned and looked up, I recognized his face and nametag. "Mark David Chapman" – John Lennon's murderer. Holy fuck! This was a true-life prisoner celebrity who killed a hero of mine. Maybe I should have exacted revenge for Lennon that day, but I didn't.

They took me out of the psych ward and moved me back to Groveland. There were two separate sides of the prison, so they moved me to the other side, away from whoever must have punched me. Sure I had to start out new there with a huge black eye, but was glad to be away from that black nutcase Jaymore.

On the other side, I got a decent job in the warehouse where everything from the outside world came through. I had access to goods and could steal things such as instant coffee and sugar. The sugar was good for making prison hooch - alcoholic drinks. Someone always had a batch of it going in their toilet. It tasted nasty but got you drunk.

I met a guy I went to high school with named Otis. Tall white kid with long dreads. He was in prison for getting caught with a few thousand hits of acid coming home from a Grateful Dead concert. He was doing 1-3 years. We played chess a lot.

One more guy had to challenge me to a fight. I was just joking around with this Venezuelan dude. Then his Spanish buddies all started egging him on - saying I disrespected him and needed to be taught a lesson. Just my luck to get a teacher who doesn't speak English.

The white supremacist guys in the prison filled me in on what was being said about the fight. They offered all sorts of weapons and protection. But I didn't take anything from them. I just knew this fight was inevitable and thought weapons would make this a much bigger prison gang altercation. The white supremacists help me, then I'd have to do shit for them and end up with a swastika carved on my forehead. That might impact any future success with Jewish guys.

I did ask the white guys to come with me in case his boys were gonna try to jump in and beat me down too. The fight was in the prison bathroom. We were standing in the dorm toilet facing each other with his Spanish boys there and the white guys behind me.

We started fighting. I struck first. I just dominated, punching him quickly in the face a few times. He didn't hit me at all man. Then the Spanish guys said the COs were coming and everyone scattered. But I don't think the COs were coming. They were just getting their boy the fuck out of there and away from the fight. That was that and nothing else was said.

* * *

Time went by slowly, and I had lots of time to think about how I never wanted to come back to prison and lose my freedom.

The COs were fucking assholes that seemed to get off on being assholes. This was 1984 and AIDS was pretty new. The prison had a medical wing where they put all the AIDS patients. A lot of guys in prison were stricken, and they were really full blown. They didn't have HIV they had AIDS.

And I could hear the COs talking shit about them real negatively. It was the middle of winter and I could hear them say how they left the windows open in the medical wing, so the prisoners with AIDS would get pneumonia and die. Left the fucking windows open in the middle of winter. They were like, "Yo, speed it along. This faggot'll be dead soon."

Ain't that fucked up? That's what they did.

I had another friend in prison I probably shouldn't have been friends with. He raped his daughter. Otherwise he was a nice guy. The day he went to the parole board, he was real excited. He was even on good terms with his daughter again and she was there to speak on his behalf for early release. But right before he walked into the parole room, he dropped dead of a heart attack.

I was waiting for him to come back and tell me the results and was excited for him. And the guards were like, "It serves that guy right for raping his daughter. He got his just rewards." The guards weren't nice people.

A few years earlier when I was in 8th grade, we had a cousin in our family killed by her boyfriend. The news described it as a satanic suicide ritual. Her boyfriend was the first to be convicted under a new assisted suicide law inspired by Dr. Jack Kevorkian.

So in prison I was friends with these three guys. One day, one of them said he wanted to tell me something. "Remember that thing with your cousin a while ago? Well I was her boyfriend at the time. I'm the guy that was with her when she was killed, and I was sent to prison for it."

Dude, the things that rushed through my head at that time were, "I need to kill this guy right now. I need revenge for my family."

I wanted to kill him right then, but was leaving on a bus to go to a new prison in an hour. So what I decided to do was talk to these Italian inmates I was tight with. I pulled them aside and said, "Guys, I'm fucking leaving right now, but this is the deal and what I found out. Can you take care of this dude for me?" They're like, "Yeah, consider it a favor." They didn't like this guy anyway.

I don't know what happened. But I'm sure these Italian guys did something. I'd seen them exact revenge on people at night.

There was this one guy who slept across from my cell. He was a white dude who came in there thinking he was all tough and was gonna take over. These Italian guys were like, "Fuck this motherfucker. He don't run shit." So in the middle of the night when the CO left the dorm to talk to the other CO, four of the Italians slipped out of their beds and went into the guy's cell. Two of them took a sheet on either side of the bed and held it down so he couldn't get up. The other two had socks filled with padlocks, tuna soup cans and batteries and beat him over the fucking face with it. Beat the living shit out of him. Muffled his cries and shit. They did it for 20 or 30 seconds. Then they all ran back to their beds. The CO didn't hear anything till the guy stumbled into the hallway bleeding.

Then for the next 30 days, the guy who got beat up was put in a segregated box that all of us could see. I thought that was pretty funny. He was the one who got beat up and he was thrown into the box. A real asshole.

So I know these Italian guys did something to that dude who helped my cousin end her own life. They were those types of guys.

Remember that guy by the Port Authority who said he wanted to hang out then raped me? The one who looked like Egon from *Ghostbusters*. I actually saw him in prison. It was at an Alcoholics Anonymous meeting and he was there as an invited outside guest of another inmate.

He just talked a lot about his own problems and addictions and helping his friend. Meanwhile, this guy was a total fucking psycho who had given me the scare of my life. I don't even think he recognized me dude. I just couldn't believe I saw him again. But I said nothing. What was I gonna say?

Some months later, I went in front of the parole board. I really wanted to get out of prison more than anything I'd ever wanted.

The parole panel asked why I thought they should let me free and what my plans were if they gave me early release. I told them I'd live with the priest I knew from back home in his guest house, get on my feet then get a job and my own place. And besides that be a productive member of society. I pointed out my good behavior in prison to show that I'd changed.

They had me leave the room while they deliberated. I was so nervous man. A couple hours later they called me back, congratulated me and said I received my parole. I thanked them and wrote a really happy letter home to my family. My time in prison had been a nightmare for them too.

CHAPTER 9

FIRED UP

I got out of prison and hooked up with that kinky slut Tess who'd been writing me sexy letters during my time away. She was lots of fun and would get into just about anything I could suggest.

I rented an apartment on Long Island just a few miles away from my hometown of Massapequa. One good thing about my legal troubles is that they actually managed to bring my family closer together. We increased our communication and cared about what happened to each other more. It was great to have a relationship again and to live close by, if not with them. I found a job working for a sanitation company.

I wanted to grow some roots in my new town. So I got the idea to join the local volunteer fire department. Even though I just got out of prison, I was able to pass their background check easily since my youthful offender status gave me a clean criminal record.

I met lots of cool guys and soon became great friends with some of them. At the fire department, we drank lots. All the time it seemed. At every department event we would drink. Every day we were drinking. Every night was drinking. Drinking, drinking, drinking. After every meeting there was cheap beer. We had a beer vending machine in the firehouse. If you were underage, you could drink there with no problem. I was already a serious alcoholic and joining the fire department turned me into an even bigger one.

Cops would hang out in the back room all the time. They would be on patrol, hide their cars behind the firehouse and drink with us. We could do anything we wanted in the town and get away with it. The cops let us slide on everything dude.

And some of the younger guys did lots of cocaine. They looked so straight-laced and preppy, but they were doing 8 balls in the station house. I never tried coke before. Then three of the young guys said they had an 8 ball. We did it a few times in my apartment. One of them would get really paranoid and start hearing things. Look outside the blinds, unlock and lock the doors dozens of times to make sure they were locked, listened for people in the hallway. Seeing people and shadows that weren't there. A real annoying type of cokehead. The other guys just chilled and did some lines.

We went on a fire department Carnival Cruise vacation to the Bahamas, flying down to Miami to catch the ship to Nassau. In JFK Airport on the way there, four of us did bumps of coke in the handicap stall in the bathroom. One of the guys dropped a little coke on the bathroom floor and it landed in a puddle of urine. He got down, picked it up with his finger and put the coke right up his nose. I saw this and thought this is a disgusting drug.

Then we did coke the whole time on the cruise. We'd do some bumps in the room, go out dancing to the clubs, party then go back to the room and do more. We brought weed with us too. A lot of guys in the department smoked weed.

There was this 68-year-old lady named Gertrude who was always at the fire department parties and events. She was the captain's aunt and head of the Ladies' Auxiliary. Just like everyone else there, Gertie was always getting drunk at these events. Then as she got drunk she would start hitting on me playfully. I'd play along and my friends would laugh.

Then after a while, I was drunk and started thinking, "I bet I could get this lady to blow me." So one night while she was flirting, I took it a step further and whispered in her ear, "Gertie, you go home right now and leave the back door open. I'll be over in about 15 minutes." She gave me a joking look. Then she could tell I was totally serious and ready to do this. Dude, five minutes later she left and 15 minutes later I left.

I went over to her house and walked in through the back door that she left open for me. I went upstairs and found

Gertrude in bed wearing a little negligee. I went in there and fucked a 68-year-old lady. And not just once.

I got Gertrude's phone number and saw her another 6 or 8 times after that. Whenever it was really late and I'd be drunk and horny, I'd call and say, "Gertie, can I come over?" She wanted me to park up the street, since she lived next door to the church choir director and didn't want him to see my car there.

I'd walk down the block, around the backyard and up the stairs, fuck her face real quick then fuck her pussy. And then I'd fucking leave. I used to hit that when I was really drunk dude. It's kind of a funny memory.

The arson wasn't as funny.

I had real mental problems back then. Real self-esteem issues and a lot of things going on. And I did something that a volunteer firefighter should never do. I lit some fires. Sometimes I'd light fires and sometimes I'd show up to help put them out.

Mind you, they were always abandoned buildings and houses. I never caused any injuries or fatalities. But I did light some fires. I don't know if it was for the excitement or just my instinct to do something bad. I was always drunk in general and drunk when I did it.

I didn't go to all the calls, because I didn't want to be suspected. You would always hear about volunteer firefighters who set the fires being the first ones on the scene. I tried not being that guy. But I probably did light like twelve fires. Which is fucked up. It was bizarre and mental shit. I think I suffered from mental disease. I had mental problems combined with alcoholism and drug use.

After a while, I knew I was under suspicion. I overheard on my police radio that they were doing a stakeout of my apartment. I went out and confronted the cops in their car. I told them they were barking up the wrong tree. And in those days, before every minute of your life was recorded, they couldn't prove anything.

I spotted arson cops tailing my car. Growing up the son of a cop and calling the cops on myself so many times taught me something about being followed. So I caught them and confronted them. They were pissed that I confronted them. I said, "Don't ever fuck with me again."

The priest I knew hooked me up with a lawyer who sent the police a letter of complaint for harassment. The letter said that if the cops wanted to contact me, they should talk to the lawyer first. They never bothered me again.

So many people stuck up for me and spoke on my behalf and in my favor.

* * *

During this time, I managed to get my first girlfriend.

Arlene was 21 and from Texas. I met her when she was working as a waitress at the bar across the street from my apartment. She was recently divorced and had the cutest 5-year-old daughter named Fern. They lived nearby with her mom and huge redneck brother. Both her mother and brother always looked real angry and mean whenever I saw them.

Arlene and I hit it off right away. I loved her personality. She was very feminine in a Texan way. We didn't even fuck until the third date. Took it slow and I found myself getting romantic with a girl for the first time. And when we did start banging, it was amazing and passionate. She gave the best blowjobs. I was in love and began thinking that maybe I wasn't gay anymore and wouldn't have to live that secret life.

Eventually I asked Arlene and Fern to move in with me. She jumped at it, as she loved me and wanted to get away from her psycho mother and brother. It was great living together and having someone to sleep with every night and being invited to love her and her daughter.

Arlene got a job selling mortgages and soon was making good money. Her boss Stanley was teaching her the business and helped with getting the proper licenses. She started having meetings with her boss after work. I thought this was fine, as Arlene had to work hard to make the money she was making, and had the realistic potential to make a lot more. After all, Stanley was 35 and began where she was in the business. Now he drove a Porsche, lived in a beautiful house in a nice neighborhood and was a self-made millionaire.

I loved being in little Fern's life. When I wasn't working my two jobs as a loss prevention agent at Sears and Marshall's, I was showering Fern with gifts, taking her to parks, the beach, the Long Island Game Farm. On Sunday mornings, I took her to an empty parking lot where she sat on my lap and steered my car. She really loved this. It was the kind of thing I wished my dad had done with me.

The sex with Arlene was nightly and I felt we had a healthy bond. A few months into the relationship, I went to surprise her at work with concert tickets to see Garth Brooks at Madison Square Garden. To get these tickets I had to wait in line for 10 hours overnight. He was her favorite singer.

I parked in the lot and saw Arlene by Stanley's jet black Porsche talking to him. I didn't want to interrupt their business discussion, so I waited for them to be done talking. Then I watched her lean in and kiss him very passionately… It was probably no more than 20 seconds but felt like a lifetime. My lifetime. They broke the kiss, got into their respective cars and drove off in the same disrespectful direction.

Tears immediately began flowing. But I collected myself and followed their cars with mine. I followed them a few miles until they got to Stanley's house and went inside. I was devastated. I felt betrayed, used and stupid. I gave her and her child all of me and trusted that her feelings for me were the same.

I went home and later got a call from Arlene telling me she would be working late. She said how sorry she was, but that she and Stanley were trying to close on a deal that would make her a really nice bonus. I said okay I understood, but revealed nothing of what I knew or saw.

Then I drove back to Stanley's house, where both cars were still in the driveway. I parked out of sight down the block. It was dark so I crept up, looking into the windows. I saw them together on a couch – with Arlene wearing just a bra and a pair of his gym shorts and Stanley shirtless in shorts. They were drinking red wine. Smooth jazz was playing on the stereo.

I cried there in his bushes and wanted to scream. I wanted to hurt him. But really it wasn't his fault. I was jealous that he was so well off and I couldn't compete. Far more damaging was Arlene's betrayal and the lying and deceitful fucking with my true emotions.

I rang the bell, not knowing what I would say or do. The curtain moved and Stanley looked outside. I could hear him through the door saying, "Oh shit, it's Joe." There was lots of shuffling on the other side.

"My Joe?"

Stanley put on a shirt and opened the door.

"Where is Arlene?" I asked.

He said she didn't want to talk to me. I said I wanted to hear that from her. Rage filled me. Rage to freak out, strike out and cause pain to him and her like they'd done to me.

Stanley said, "One minute," and closed the door. He came back and said I needed to leave his property before they called the police, and that Arlene would call me in a couple hours when I calmed down. He could see the rage and fury growing inside me.

I turned to walk away. As I passed Arlene's car, I made a fist and punched the driver's side window, knocking the glass out. Glass shattered about and blood gushed from my hand. With my bleeding hand in great pain, I got in my car and peeled off like a maniac, thinking about how I was going to make them suffer for doing this to me.

A week later, Arlene called and said she wanted to pick up her and Fern's clothes. I said I'd load it all in my car and meet her in the parking lot of a local diner. I went, saw her there and she didn't apologize and run back to me like I hoped she would. She just coldly asked if it was all there. I said yes then stopped her.

"How the fuck do you get off using me like you did and lying to me when I gave all of myself to you and your daughter?"

Arlene told me she fell in love with Stanley and that was that.

Rage! Fury! Never had I done this before and I felt immediately guilty after, but I bitch-smacked Arlene real hard against her left cheek. Almost knocked her over, but she caught herself on my car. She recovered, stared at me and cried as I said I was sorry. Arlene took her stuff and drove off, moving in with Stanley and becoming vice president of the mortgage company.

From that point on, I had major trust issues with women.

I felt totally betrayed. I started pining away and thinking back to all the other times I'd been hurt in life. My mind kept hovering over the first woman who betrayed me. My birth mother, who sent me away from her life on my first day.

Who was she?

CHAPTER 10

MAMA BOOTS

Growing up, I always knew I was adopted. I always felt weird. Always felt different. I felt that I was given away. Why was I given away? Maybe my parents didn't love me.

When you're a little kid, you don't think about being grateful to the people who took you in and shared their life with you. Any time I fought with my parents, I fantasized about what it would be like growing up with the family that gave me up. I fantasized about that a lot.

My parents used to say, "You should tell people you're special and that we got to pick you. We got to choose you." I actually told people this.

It was depressing.

What I really hated was when people would walk up to me when I was with my parents and say, "He looks just like you," because we did kind of look similar. And I'd be thinking, "I don't look like them. I'm not of them." Every time someone said that it really fucked with my head.

Where did I come from?

So at the age of 21 I was like I'm really gonna try and find my birth mother.

So I began researching about how to find your parents. Through the library, I found out that New York State will give adoptees non-identifying information about their birth mothers. This includes religion, age, ancestry, height, weight, eye color and pertinent medical information. That type of stuff. So I sent away and got all of that info.

Then I started using my head and said to myself, "You know what? When I was born at that Catholic hospital in the Bronx, I bet I was baptized there and that there's a baptismal certificate with my original name on it." Not only that - I bet I had an original birth certificate that was later amended. But I had no idea what my name could have been.

So I went to the NYC Public Library – the big one with those stoned lions in front. A librarian helped me find a giant book of all the 1967 Bronx births. Then I tried to match them with the numbers on my birth certificate. I went through this book for hours. Finally I matched it up man. With the number I did a cross-reference. It said "Gregory Leonard Nelson" and it was my birth certificate.

Gregory Leonard Nelson. I found out who I was.

So I had this much information. Now I had to find out who my mother was, which would still be difficult. I took a chance and called Our Lady of Mercy Hospital, where I was born.

I called up and said, "Hi, my name is Gregory Leonard Nelson. I'm getting married in a few months and I'm looking for a copy of my baptismal certificate. Do you have a copy?"

The lady on the phone went to look. She said, "We do have it on record here. You were baptized here. Would you want me to mail it to you?"

"Actually, I'm in the neighborhood today. I could stop by and pick it up."

She said, "Sure, come on by." Then she added, "By the way, you're not an adoptee looking for your birth mother, are you?"

I'm like oh fuck and began getting nervous.

"No, why?"

She said because they did a lot of adoptions through this hospital back then. "Now and then we get people coming to look for their birth mothers and we can't give out that information."

I repeated my story about getting married etc. She said yeah that's fine, come on by. A couple hours later I took the train up to the Bronx. I went in and spoke to a nun working in the office. She gave me a coffee, took out this big book and found all my information. She began transcribing a new baptismal certificate.

Then I purposely spilled coffee all over myself and made a big scene. I apologized, but she said not to worry. The nun left the office to get stuff to clean up the mess.

I had a mere few seconds and ran over to her desk. I looked down real quick at the certificate and saw the name just before she came back in the office.

Judith Nelson.

Now I had my mother's name. What was next?

From the background information I got from NY State, I knew she grew up in Brooklyn. I also knew her age back when I was born in 1967 and had some basic descriptions of her looks.

I went back to the NYC library and went to the third floor, where they had phone directories going back to the 1880s. So I looked through the 1967 phone books. Nelson. There were tons of Nelsons. So I decided to call all the Nelsons in the phone book.

I started dialing and dialing for hours and days. Calling Nelsons, giving the pitch. "Hi, I know this call might sound unusual. My name is Joseph. I'm trying to find my birth mother Judith Nelson. She was 18 years old in the year 1967; she gave me up for adoption. She looked like this at that age. Do you maybe know who she is?"

A lot of people said, "No, sorry I can't help you." Then others were like, "What kind of scam are you running?"

On the third day of doing this, I got this girl on the phone, talked to her and gave her my usual spiel. "You know what?" she suddenly said. "That sounds a lot like my Aunt Judy!"

I go, "Really?" She goes, "Yeah, let me talk to my mother. She might know." She told me to call back in a couple hours.

So I called back later that night. This time, a guy got on the phone and said, "Listen motherfucker, I don't know what kind of scam you're running, but don't ever fucken call here again. If you do, I'm gonna fucken lay a hurting on you."

I said, "Dude, I'm not running any scam." But he hung up on me.

Fuck. Fuck!

I waited a few hours. Then I said fuck it. I made it this far. So I called again. This time a woman answered.

"Joseph?" She said, "I'm glad you called back. I'm sorry about my son. He didn't know. He thought you were running a scam. I think you found your birth mother, and I think I'm your Aunt Nora."

Nora started telling me the story of the adoption. She said that back then, her little sister Judith became pregnant twice. It was such an embarrassment to the family that she was unmarried and pregnant, they told relatives and friends Judith was on California vacations. She was really up in the Bronx with the nuns waiting to give birth out of sight. They even had Judith write postcards from Hollywood and Disneyland and showed people. This was the way they did it back in the 1960s. It was a real shame to be a single mother and to be pregnant back then. Abortion was illegal.

She said, "Listen, give me a day or two to talk to Judith and find out how this is gonna go."

I hung up and fell to tears the entire night. After everything I'd been through in life, I saw finding my mother as my salvation and a chance to start down a new path.

Nora called me back the next day. She said, "Are you sitting down? Judy's your mother. At first she was startled. She wanted to know what you wanted, what you were looking for. Money…"

I said definitely not. I just wanted to look for who I was and where I came from, and wouldn't ask for any money. I was willing to forgive the last 21 years of missed allowances.

Through my Aunt Nora, my mother and I arranged to meet at a bar in Bay Ridge, Brooklyn. I got there two hours early. The old Italian bartender and waitress were so touched by the situation as I told them the whole story and how nervous and excited I was.

Finally it was time. I went outside the bar to wait. I saw a woman walking out of the train and immediately knew it was her.

She came close and it was the first time I ever saw my face in someone else's face. This was a weird experience at the age of 21.

We hugged and cried right there in the street. We walked into the bar, and all eyes in that place were on us. All night the drinks were free. I could see the old bartender crying. It was real emotional for him, my birth mother and me.

And we talked. We must have talked for hours. What do you do? Where have you been living? What have you been doing? Where we grew up, our parents, how we were brought up. She asked about my older brother Vinnie, who she had named Andrew. She was comforted that we both went to the same adoptive parents.

Then she told me about her life. She worked for the Department of Sanitation in their main office and lived in Bensonhurst. A couple years after she had me, she got married. He recently passed away. During their marriage they had two kids that they kept. So I had a half-brother James and half-sister Lorraine that I never met.

About a week later, I went over to her apartment and she introduced me to James and Lorraine as a coworker's son. Meanwhile, I was looking at my half-brother and thinking he had to know something. I looked just like him. James was 6 years younger and 3 inches taller but looked just like me dude. We were like twins. But it didn't click with him.

At the end of the night, she sat them down and told them that in her past she had two other kids that she gave up for adoption. Then she introduced me as their brother.

I was welcomed into the family. My mom, James and Lorraine all welcomed me. It was special. They were happy to have two new brothers in me and my other brother Vinnie, who they eventually did meet. I just thought it was really cool.

I arranged for my parents to meet with my birth mother. My parents don't drink, but she wanted to meet them at a bar. My parents asked if she knew anything about my birth father. Could she at least give them his name?

"Yeah, Jack Daniels," she said.

My new half-siblings James and Lorraine were under-age teenagers at the time, but she let them drink. It was not a problem for her how much or how often they drank. She was a complete alcoholic; her kids were complete alcoholics. The whole family was complete alcoholics. They had beer cans on their Christmas tree as decorations.

All the cousins and aunts, everybody loved to drink. It was a drinking family. Her parents had both died of alcoholism and mental disease. They were locked in institutions and mental hospitals. So there was mental illness and alcoholism running rampant in the family. At least I inherited something.

Then I actually moved in with them for a while. I slept on a blow up mattress in my half-brother's bedroom. It was great to finally be living with my real family. This was what I always dreamed of growing up. And we all got along well.

About a month after I moved in, the Fourth of July came around. We were outside that night drinking and having fun. Then my mom started saying the stupidest shit to me, and I started saying stupid shit back. I was talking to her neighbors and mentioned some guys up the street.

She said, "You don't know shit."

I'm like, "What the fuck are you talking about?"

She said, "You don't know shit about nobody. You talk like you know people around here."

"What are you talking about?"

She started with her mouth and I was like you know what? Fuck you. She said fuck you. We had a big argument and really went at it. We were both drunk. I packed up my shit in my bags. I was like, "Fuck you I never want to see you again."

I took all my bags, left the apartment, went downstairs, stormed through the basement laundry room and slammed open the back door of the building. A black family was entering from the other side and I almost knocked them over with the door.

"Hey, watch what you doing!" the father shouted at me. But I just kept going and didn't say shit.

It was Fourth of July night and therefore really hard to get a cab and get the fuck out of there. My half-brother James came out crying and said, "Joey, what happened? Why did you do this?" I'm like, "Dude, I didn't do nothing. I'm sorry. I love you man." Dejected, sad and angry, he went back inside, leaving me alone.

Just then, the black guy whose family I almost hit with the door rolled up in a car with two other guys. They got out of the car and beat the shit out of me on Cropsy Avenue. They left me for dead in the middle of the street.

I woke up 15 hours later in Coney Island Hospital with a black eye and contusion under my ear. I was a mess. But I still had my bags with me in the hospital room. The cops found me in the middle of the street. I was unconscious from the alcohol and beating and had been in a coma.

My birth mother never knew what happened. There was no hospital reunion. I never saw or heard from her again. My mother's been out of my life for 20 years now and I don't miss her.

I woke up in the hospital surrounded by my mother and family. My real family. The Bootsolinos. My father said, "I don't know what happened to you, but we gotta get you out of here."

So I went to California.

CHAPTER 11

WEST COAST ROMP

After that pummeling, my father bought me a plane ticket to Los Angeles to get away from the craziness. I'd never been to the West Coast, but had a friend Ray who just moved out there. I was also intrigued by the thought of a more laid back atmosphere and showbiz culture.

I stayed at Ray's apartment in Burbank while healing from my Brooklyn injuries. Then I got my own place in Los Angeles. Now I was a real California Gurl.

I started taking acting classes and auditioned for parts in plays, TV shows and movies. I was in the drama *A View From the Bridge* by Arthur Miller and played a character named Submarine. A small role but it was a well-reviewed play. And it was just cool to be part of something and work with a team of people towards a common goal like that.

I also got work as an extra in movies and on television shows. No lines or anything but I would get $75 to $100 a day, free meals and the chance to hang out on movie sets.

Talk Dirty After Dark starring Martin Lawrence. You can see me sitting behind Martin on the bus in that movie. Remember that show *Life Goes On* with the mentally challenged kid Corky? I played a soldier in that. On *The Flash* TV series I was an ambulance attendant. On *Father Dowling Mysteries* I was a Chicago police officer.

After all that extra work and auditioning, I finally landed a starring role on a major daytime TV show. I was a real-life plaintiff on *The People's Court*. This was when the show had Judge Wapner and Rusty the Bailiff.

Back when I was looking for my own place, this young 20-something girl named Pamela sublet her apartment to me for a few months. She said she needed the cash and deposit upfront. But when I went to move in, the landlord said Pamela was getting evicted and had no business subletting this place to anyone. He said I was the second guy today to show up and fall for her scam.

I looked in the building dumpster out back and found a bunch of her things in trash bags. I emptied the bags out in the driveway and looked through her notes. Through that, I learned she was moving to her mother's house and even found the address scribbled on a piece of paper. I called the cops and they arrested her ass.

An officer later called me and said that Pamela's mother was willing to pay the amount she ripped me off if I dropped the charges. The cops recommended this, as they said it would take forever if I went through the courts. So I should just take her mother's money then if I wanted I could sue her in small claims court for expenses incurred. So that's what I did.

The People's Court producers were culling through case dockets and thought our situation looked interesting. They sent me a letter asking if I'd like to have my case arbitrated by Judge Wapner.

What was great was that if Judge Wapner ruled for the plaintiff, the show would pay you the settlement amount. Because a lot of times in real civil court, even when you win, the defendant doesn't even pay and just claims they're indigent. That also entices the defendant to go on because the show ponies up.

So we went on *The People's Court* and I easily won my case. It went much better than my last court trial. And I was on TV.

I also began prank calling Los Angeles radio shows. Like former LA police chief Daryl Gates, who had a show on AM radio. He was the chief in charge during the Rodney King beating and LA riots. A real militant asshole police chief. I would call his show and start out by asking a serious question. Then I'd flip it up and start cursing him off. Very juvenile and fun.

I got a job at a gay phone sex hotline. I saw an ad in the paper, so I went in and they tested me out. One of the guys who worked there called and I talked dirty sex to him. This was different from most job interviews.

It was a real seedy place. I was nervous for the first couple of calls but then got into it. I thought of it as fun and said to myself, "Look I'm acting."

When a guy called, I would start by asking him what he wanted to do. Anything to keep him on the phone for $2.99 a minute. I'd put on a young teenage voice and be like, "Hi, my name is Tyler. I have blond hair and a smooth swimmers body," as if I was a young kid. That turned these guys on like crazy. I'd hear heavy breathing and know they were having fun with themselves. Sometimes I'd be touching myself too if the call was particularly hot. Not too many workplaces would allow this.

There was this cute kid who worked on a phone across from me - this skinny little twink named Jesse. Jesse was maybe a little too much on the feminine side for me but really cute. He'd sometimes say to me, "Joey, lets go fuck around in the bathroom." But I'd always turn him down.

Then one night I watched Jesse go into the bathroom and suddenly got the urge. I hung up the phone and followed him. When he finished peeing and turned around, I was right there behind him. I reached for his cock, grabbed it and pulled him towards me. I started making out with him. Next thing I knew he was dropping to his knees and started sucking my dick. Then he came up and I started sucking his. And he had a huge dick for a little kid. We fucked around a few times after that and got together at his place. I fucked him and he fucked me.

There was also this Mexican kid I met while doing phone sex. He was only 20 and was really cute. We used to go to a gay club called Rage on Santa Monica Boulevard in West Hollywood. And we fucked around man. Giving head, making out, dancing. Hanging out with all his friends. His name was Jose.

One night after a fun night at Rage with Jose, I was walking down Santa Monica Blvd. A group of four obviously drunk white dudes on the sidewalk started messing with me, calling me a faggot and pushing me around, looking for a response.

I just kept walking and wanted to get away. Then one of them pushed and tripped me from behind. I fell down as he and his friends called me a cocksucking faggot and asked how I'd like to suck their cocks. I got up and ran away.

I made it a few blocks then saw they hadn't bothered chasing me. I slowed down and gathered my wits. I was embarrassed and pissed and wanted revenge.

I walked to the other side of the street, slowly making my way back to the scene of my humiliation, lurking in the shadows. I spotted them on a side street sitting on apartment steps. They were hard to miss as their loud, drunken shouts gave away their location.

I peeped the name of the side street then walked a block to where there was a payphone. I called 911 and said there were 4 gangbangers on my block, two of whom were brandishing pistols and that they were sitting at the corner of such and such and Santa Monica. I hung up and waited.

Not two minutes later, three marked sheriff cars rolled up on these punks, guns drawn, and ordered their drunk gay-bashing asses to the ground. After searching them and finding no weapons, they all got tickets for open containers. When the cops ran their names for warrants, two of them - including the guy who tripped me - were cuffed and hauled away.

Why didn't I just call the cops and report them for assaulting me? I was scared because I was still very much in the closet and afraid anyone would find out. I feared that in reporting it I'd have to admit I was gay to straight cops, who I knew from experience didn't think too kindly of gays.

*   *   *

After a while, I just got bored and burnt out in LA. I wandered around a little and ended up in Las Vegas. I worked as a waiter at Bally's Casino in the old MGM building doing the 10 p.m. to 6 a.m. shift. I tried it there and lasted maybe a month and a half. It was just too wild for me. My coworkers and I would get off work in the morning then all go drink across the street at another casino. Employees weren't allowed to be seen drinking at Bally's. We'd say, "This is our night time!"

Doing that just felt so wrong. To be making almost no money then spend it all on booze with these losers. I had to get out of that town.

I took a bus up to Seattle and rented a place in Pike Place Market, right by the waterfront. Seattle was a beautiful city. Very laid back and I loved going out, seeing live music and meeting people. This was the early '90s when the grunge scene was exploding out there.

I was walking around Pike Place and saw a poster advertising fishing jobs in Alaska. So I went up to this part of Seattle called Ballard where they had all the fishing company offices and boats. I hit up different companies and filled out applications. In one of the offices, I flirted a lot with a girl who worked there. I suspect she bumped up my application because I got a call from them the next day. They asked if I could come in and take a piss test. I was pretty clean during that time, so I passed.

Going up to Alaska seemed like it would be a fun adventure. And the pay was really good.

Soon I found myself on the frigid seas of Alaska on a fishing ship. This ship was a floating processor. My job was to sort and process the fish. Sort them, pan them, freeze them, bag them, stow them.

We had six fishing vessels. Whenever there was a net full of fish, we cast off a line with a buoy and hook and caught each other's nets. They'd release it and we reeled it in. A ramp dropped down from our ship to gather the fish and we'd raise it on the boom and dump all the fish out into huge holes. The fish then went onto conveyors, which had three giant tanks. All the fish we didn't want stayed on the conveyor and were shot out the side of the ship back into the water.

I had to sort through the fish and put them in large tanks. Halibut, cod, bottom fish, rockfish, flounder. It was rough - the most miserable job I ever had. It was cold, long hours. Miserable.

I wound up feeling extremely sick and fucked up on this boat in the Bering Sea. Definitely not the best place to catch a cold. I didn't know what I had, but was up all night coughing. I pleaded with the bosses to let me go inland to see a doctor, but they kept me out there for three days before dropping me off at an island that had a medical clinic. Doctors there diagnosed me with bilateral pneumonia. I was in danger of dying. They put me on a Medevac helicopter and flew me to a hospital in Anchorage, where I stayed until I recovered.

When I got back to Seattle, I began working a comp case against the fishing company for taking so long to get me medical help. The company offered me a $10,000 check to settle. Case closed. I bought some really good stocks and turned $10,000 into $17,000 in less than a year investing in tech stocks. Shit was easy.

I ended up back in Los Angeles with even less going on than before. Bored and burnt out again. Even being a thousandaire didn't do much to lift my spirits.

I was thinking a lot about what happened to me so far on this planet. I'd been a truant kid, a burglar, street hustler, arsonist and now a failed fisherman. So far my greatest accomplishment was causing people misery through my pranks and crimes.

My life was lacking something – a life. I kept thinking there must be something else out there. Something I hadn't tried.

I couldn't think of anything. So I joined the Army.

CHAPTER 12

THE FUCKING ARMY

Yeah, I did join the Army because I wanted to give back. But the main reason was that I had nothing going on for myself. I had few skills or prospects. I also wanted to do something honorable and felt joining the military would make my parents proud. And when I told them, my family was happy because they knew I would be safe for a while and out of trouble. It would be a challenge to me. It would mean discipline and getting in shape.

This was 1992. I was 25.

I flew out to Fort Jackson in South Carolina and did my 8 weeks of Basic Training there. I was nervous getting started because of the physical part and wondered if I could succeed in such a structured environment. I never thought that I could do Basic Training, but I did it. It was all mental. And the physical part anybody can do. They build you up and make you into a soldier.

After that, I went home to New York for Christmas vacation. When the break was over, I would be reporting to Fort Lee in Virginia to start my real Army service. But there was nothing going on at home. So I decided to save some vacation time and arrive at Fort Lee a week early. I also figured the military base would be chilled out with almost everybody away on holiday.

On my way down to Virginia flying out of the Philly airport, the airline employees saw my uniform and bumped me up to first class. Then I spotted another soldier there. As I walked up to him, I noticed he was a fucking two-star general. I was just a low-ranking private. Turned out he was a general at Fort Lee and was heading down there as well.

Even though he outranked me, the general ended up being really nice. He gave me a ride to the base, asked me about myself and took me where I needed to report. He even carried my bags and walked in with me to verify we were in the right place. Imagine being the sergeant at the front desk of my barracks and in walks a new recruit followed by a general carrying the recruit's bags.

"Is he in good hands, Sergeant?" the general asked.

"Yes sir."

I remember that moment fondly, because I finally felt like I found a place where people looked out for me and wanted me to be there.

"Okay, you guys have a good night."

* * *

My Army battalion went to Bosnia in December 1995. We were excited because we'd been training for a year and a half for this mission and knew eventually we were gonna go.

The three republics had just signed a peace accord in Dayton, Ohio. I was part of the US and international mission to keep peace between the fighting factions of the former Yugoslavia.

The first day over there, my troop was crossing the Slava River in Croatia. Our lead scout, an E-7 staff sergeant, discovered a personnel mine. He decided he was gonna diffuse it himself instead of calling the Explosive Ordnance Disposal technicians. So he took a pair of pliers, a knife and screwdriver and tried using those to diffuse the thing. It exploded in his face and he was found off the road with shrapnel stuck in his head.

He was the first casualty on the first day. It was a really dangerous place and there were lots of landmines. They called it the land of six million landmines. Three of my friends got blown up. They all survived though. It was dangerous.

My regiment was part of the effort to keep the formerly warring sides apart. The Russians were like, "This is a NATO thing, but we're gonna be involved in this too." So the Russians were in our sector.

My first job there was to be an Army cook. We cooked in combat conditions in bombed-out buildings in the middle of winter. I was responsible for feeding about 18 men.

There was this black sergeant I worked for, Sergeant Jenkins. He hated me and I hated him. He just rode my dick most of the time. Now I love my black brothers and sisters man, but this guy was a racist. He hated white people. And we just got into it.

But I didn't let him fuck with me. Sergeant Jenkins was from down South and had a thick southern accent. I played real stupid when he was talking, pretending I couldn't understand him. I thought that was a legitimate way to fuck with someone without getting in trouble. I'd be like, "I'm sorry Sergeant, but I couldn't understand what you just said," while he got increasingly irate.

He made my life there hell and we were always butting heads. I just kept pissing him off, mostly by pointing out things he was doing wrong. Jenkins was violating Army rules by sleeping in the same trailer where we served food. And right behind the serving counter just out of sight from where people ate, Jenkins had a piss jug filled with a few night's worth of stale urine. He didn't even empty it out during the day. I thought that was pretty disgusting and told him on the sly that he should get rid of it. He just told me to mind my own business and kept filling up the urine jug.

Later when he was on the food line with some other officers, I loudly said, "Sergeant Jenkins, you might want to get rid of that piss jug you have behind the counter. Its not very sanitary." I called him out right in front of the officers. They looked at him with shock and disgust. His face went from black to red.

And he was even more pissed at me after that. Jenkins tried writing me up a few times, but nothing ever stuck. He would talk shit about me to subordinate soldiers. People that I outranked, which wasn't good to do in a regiment. Because then they also thought they could talk shit to me.

The principle mission of my Army battalion was to prevent fighting between the Bosnian Muslims and ethnic Albanians, which meant keeping all sides of the conflict apart. It was a pretty challenging mission because the anger was still raw on all sides.

We set up different zones for the different ethnic groups to live with checkpoints all over. I was in a tank brigade. We did patrols all day, sometimes going on specific missions but mostly just showing our presence in the area.

My battalion was kept in pretty squalid conditions until getting a new, bigger base built by the Halliburton company. At the new quarters, the Army replaced us with Scottish cooks. I didn't have a permanent job anymore, so I became Johnny Soldier. What's that? Basically it was everything besides combat. Guard duty, supply runs, watch and checkpoint patrols.

I went on patrols through the villages with civilian affairs teams, military intelligence and CIA guys. Those guys would try to make contact and become friendly with village leaders and local politicians. I'd be pulling security. And I got to meet a lot of people. The kids would come running out to see us. I met the village moonshiners making homemade booze. And our superiors actually encouraged us to have a couple shots of moonshine with them if we wanted. They said that might build more camaraderie and gain the respect and support of the locals. So I made sure to have a few shots, or probably more than a few.

From talking to people and the kids there, I learned that the village schools were in bad shape. Now I was never a big fan of school myself, but these kids really wanted to go and learn. But they had nothing in their school and they would just go a couple hours a day if at all. They didn't have materials or supplies to work with.

So I wrote home about it, and my mother told my aunt who worked in the administrator's office of a school district on Long Island. My aunt helped organize a relief drive in the district for school supplies to be sent to Bosnian kids. I was soon inundated with packages and packages filled with supplies.

So I got with the local chaplain and civilian affairs guys and distributed the donations to local schools. It made me feel really good to help these kids. They were so grateful to get some pens and crayons, rulers. We had the rulers in centimeters and inches. And writing pads you know? It was just nice to be able to give them something.

Then the school supply drive started getting bigger and more organized. Soon I was collecting donations from two major charity organizations. Then I found out one of these charity groups was secretly smuggling weapons to the refugees in their school supplies packages. These organizations had ways to fast-track packages so they wouldn't get checked. So I found out about it, but I didn't say nothing. I wasn't trying to fuck with militias or get myself implicated.

They even put together a charity concert in New York for this organization. Yoko Ono and Sean Lennon performed, not realizing that this supposedly peaceful group for refugees was actually smuggling weapons in their care packages.

* * *

There was this one guy in my Bosnian unit who always seemed gay to me. He was just so sweet. Skinny little white dude. Everybody said he's got just a little too much sugar in his blood.

I followed him to his room one day and said, "Dude, I know you're fucking gay."

"What made you know?"

"All you gotta do is open your mouth. How would you like to fuck me and suck my dick?"

He was like, "Fuck yeah girlfriend!"

Dude, we were doing it in the bunk bed with my legs up in the air and he was pounding away at me. That was me in a bed in the barracks. But we couldn't be too loud about it. Getting caught doing gay stuff would get you discharged.

*　*　*

Out on the field I would be up in the fucking tank, driving around the Serb sector with a fully loaded 240 machine gun on a tank. I'd go out with scouts in their Humvees. These were things I never thought I would ever do. I wrote to that great teacher from Catholic school Mrs. Greene, telling her everything I was doing and how she inspired me to do good things in the world. Then I got a letter from her family saying she recently passed away.

I saw some crazy things in Bosnia. Helped dig up mass graves full of dead civilians dumped there by the other side. Skeletons of men, women and children in civilian clothing with their hands tied behind their backs, showing signs of torture.

I saw prisoner exchanges. These guys who'd been in POW camps for years were exchanged between the Muslims and Serbs. I saw their faces as they gained freedom. Watched joyful families as they reunited with loved ones they thought they'd never see again.

I went on the first US-Russia joint patrol since 1945 in Berlin. We had spies and CIA with us on our base and they had KGB spies with them. So we all hung out, but we had to be careful about what we said.

We built our barracks at the end of a road that separated two villages whose residents hated each other. The village on one side was where the Bosnian Muslims lived. Ethnic Albanian Serbs lived on the other side. The problem was that the Muslims used to live on the other side of the road. The Serbs kicked them out and massacred them in incidents that the UN would later declare international war crimes. Genocide. So emotions were raw. There were World War One-style trenches on both sides of the road.

During the day, the Muslims would go into the Serb village because they knew we would protect them. They'd start rebuilding their old houses. Then every night, Serbs would blow up those houses. One night we were sleeping in our tents and probably six houses in a row blew up. And everybody went out looking. That was an exciting night.

The Muslims would also go back to the Serb village during the day, go to the cemeteries and dig up the bodies of their dead relatives. They wanted to rebury them in their new village. One of the things I had to do at the checkpoint was have people open coffins so I could check the bodies and skulls to see if they were smuggling weapons or explosives. I felt terrible doing that. I felt like I was violating people's relatives.

One day I was walking around the base doing my usual patrols and security. Just then, a Navy jet fighter doing a practice run accidentally dropped a real bomb on our fucking camp. A 500-pound bomb right on the edge of our camp! It sent shrapnel all over. Nobody got hit. Guys had soda cans with shrapnel torn up from it and shit. Our own Navy dropped a bomb on us.

This little Bosnian Muslim kid from the village used to hang around our base. We called him Elvis because of the rock concert shirts he always wore. A bunch of those shirts had been donated by aid organizations. One of the officers even managed to get a purple jumpsuit for little Elvis to wear.

Well one day these Serbian police officers told Elvis there was candy in a bag, and to go get it if he wanted it. The bag exploded. I saw the kid about a month later and his arm was all fucked up. Elvis.

Otherwise, it was mostly a peace mission. After Bosnia, I was stationed as a cook in the nearby nation of Macedonia. Our base was outside the capital city Skopje near the main airport.

The US was in Macedonia to observe the border of Kosovo and Serbia and to oversee the area from the mountains. They also wanted to protect the country, which was a breakaway of Yugoslavia, from being taken over by the Serbs. The Serbs didn't want Yugoslavia breaking up. This is kind of confusing, isn't it? If there's any place in the world that needs to be fenced in and just have their borders decided already it's these fucken countries.

So we were up on the mountains and had outposts watching the border for ammunition smuggled from Albania into

Kosovo, especially after the revolution when Albania took over the armory and stole all the weapons. We would find donkey convoys concealing loads of ammunition.

I worked in the battalion kitchen as a nighttime baker. I'd go to work at 6 p.m. and make all the cakes, pies, cookies and stuff like that. Baked goods. It was a fun job because I liked cooking, baking and eating!

We had some locals working with us in the kitchen. Every day they'd bring me either a bottle of local wine or this homemade booze called Rakia. Good, strong moonshine. Shit was like 40-60% alcohol. Man I used to get drunk every fucken night then be off in the morning.

There was this one girl in the battalion who was pretty hot for an Army chick. I started fucking around with her. We got it on in the kitchen pantry. That didn't last too long though. She wound up finding an officer to fuck. I was a cook, a corporal. Fraternization is against military rules, but nobody knew.

A diplomat on our base from the US embassy told me about a hotel where you could get hookers in Skopje. We were allowed to go into the city whenever we weren't working. It was a very safe place.

So when I got a pass, I went into Skopje and found the hotel. The diplomat gave detailed instructions about what to do when I got there. It wasn't too complicated. I approached the desk clerk and said I wanted a girl in my room.

"What kind of girl?" he asked.

"A beautiful, dark-haired girl with big tits."

He told me to go to my room and she would be there in a half hour. $125 for two hours.

I went up, and it was actually a beautiful room in a nice hotel. Not seedy at all. Soon there was a knock at the door and I opened it. The girl was gorgeous. She was 17-18 and had long dark hair. And just a beautiful, curvy body.

She came in the room and we took a shower together. She had no qualms about making out. I started kissing her heavily and led her to the bed, straddled her face and had her suck my cock. Before I came, I stuck it in her pussy and just started fucking her. I came pretty quickly then laid down and snuggled with her a little bit, sucking her tits.

I got hard again and fucked her again. Then I pulled it out right before I came, squirted in her face and in her mouth, made her eat it. Snuggled with her again. This happened a few times. It was nice being with somebody like that and just laying down together. Holding her tight, naked. Nice and relaxing.

Then the two hours were up and I said thank you. We both cleaned up, got dressed and came out. The desk clerk gave her a cut of the money.

After Macedonia, I was stationed in Friedberg, Germany working in the kitchens. That was Ray Barracks - the same base where Elvis Presley served during his stint in the Army. The barber who cut the King's hair cut mine. He had pictures and clippers in a display case and was the local Elvis historian.

It was in Germany where I had my second taste of gay Army sex. One night, this other soldier was really drunk in my room and gave me a wet willy by licking his finger then putting it in my ear. Then I gave him a wet willy back. He stuck his finger in my mouth and I stuck my finger in his mouth. Then he just looked at me and licked my finger. I traced his lips.

Then I took his chin with my two fingers and pulled him towards me. We just started making out man. It just happened you know? And the next thing I knew we were ripping our fatigues off and 69ing on the bed, sucking each other off. He rolled me over and licked my ass.

He asked if I wanted to get fucked. I said, "Hell yeah." He made sure the doors were locked and shut the windows and blinds. The dude looked kind of funny walking naked around the room. He had some sort of skin condition and was kind of blotchy.

Then he came back to the bed and fucked me. He fucked me real good and lasted a long time, like 25 minutes, which gave me a good fucking. He came in me, pulled out and then just held me there spooning. He was talking real loving to me. He was saying, "I love you. I love you so much. This is beautiful." Those words made me feel really good.

But in Germany, I started getting in trouble and wasn't getting along with another one of the sergeants. I guess I just don't respond well to authority. I also had problems with drinking and fighting. Fighting with other soldiers. Drunken brawls if I didn't like somebody.

One night in nearby Frankfort, I went out drinking with a few of my soldier friends to this place called Sachsenhausen frequented by Americans. One of my friends was a Hispanic soldier from California. Well he got into a fight with a soldier from another base and stabbed the guy, leaving him bloody on the floor. Then we took off. He had blood all over his clothes and shit. When we got back to the base, I took his clothes to hide the evidence.

The guy got arrested by the MPs and charged with assault. He got court-martialed and we all testified. I lied and said that he was with me the whole time at the base. He was found innocent. A few months later, the same soldier went back home to Los Angeles and murdered two gang bangers. He was arrested and got life in prison. So by getting him off for the first offense, I indirectly got two other people killed. Sorry.

* * *

By the time they sent me back to a US base, I was just so stressed and burnt out from the Army. With fewer responsibilities and less distractions, my memories of Bosnia started hitting me hard.

I was burnt out and felt bad every day. Dude, everything I went through. There was a lot of fucking stress man. A lot of long hours, wearing boots all day and night. My feet still hurt all the time from that. I ended up having arthritis in both feet and residual cold weather injuries, with my limbs getting numb at odd moments.

I got sick in the Army, mentally ill. I had mental problems. I was really depressed and couldn't even do my job or cook anymore. I had really bad anxiety, was crying all the time and just couldn't function. So I went to see the Army shrink and just started breaking down as soon as I got in the shrink's office. I'm like I am so stressed out. I've been either in the field training or on high stress deployments for the last couple of years, and I'm stressed out with drinking and depression and anxiety and panic attacks. I said I couldn't function anymore man. They told me I had PTSD – post-traumatic stress disorder - and bipolar disorder.

I just wanted to leave the Army with a medical discharge. The sergeants gave me a hard time and tried to have me dishonorably discharged by making up poor performance records. I said that's BS and called up my congressman from Long Island, Peter King. I spoke to a secretary in his office and told her the deal. They sent an investigation team.

Soon after that, I was summoned to the general's office and they said I was getting an honorable discharge. I was free. This was August 10, 1998. Thank you Rep. Peter King!

It wasn't the best ending, but overall I appreciate my time spent in the Army. And I think I served my country well. Did I earn a gold or silver star? No, I didn't get any of that. But I earned an Army Achievement award, a Meritorious Service Medal, a medal for serving overseas and achieved Expert Rifleman status. There was a Bosnian award whatever that was. A NATO award for Bosnian deployment. No, I didn't get White House honors but there's a drawer in my parents' house with some bling and badges.

I drove back to Long Island, went home and slept.

CHAPTER 13

RADIO CHICK

After the Army, I set out on a path that led me to General Howard Stern.

I got discharged and stayed with my parents for a couple of weeks. Then I moved to an apartment in nearby Bethpage. The new place was just a block away from my favorite bar Mr. Beery's. After spending years doing strange things in strange places, it felt good to be home and in walking distance from a good drinking spot.

They tested us for pot in the Army, so I quickly started smoking again. I missed weed. I wasn't really pursuing a job. I put in for VA disability and was waiting for that to come through. Besides that, I had about $20,000 in the bank and was living off that. Just chilling out.

In my free time – which was all the time - I started listening to local radio shows like the Howard Stern Show and others in New York. Before I went to LA, I was listening to Stern and watching his local Channel 9 TV show on

Saturday nights. I was just drawn to his style and humor. He said whatever he wanted about sex and society, pushed the censors and fucked with famous people, all while being funny as hell. And just putting on a great show every day.

And as I listened more to Howard Stern on the K-Rock radio station, I started saying to myself - you know what man? I gotta try calling in. Cause I kept listening and I'd have funny things to say about this and that, and could say something about that person and always had something funny in mind.

So I called. But it was really hard getting through. Just busy signals, or it would keep ringing and then morph into a busy signal. Cell phones have pretty much wiped out busy signals and I don't miss them at all.

So I put the show's number on speed dial. I redialed and redialed and redialed and… (I had lots of time on my hands)

Eventually someone picked up. It was Stuttering John Melendez. A former intern who gained notoriety for his speech impediment, John was now a Stern Show producer and the phone call gatekeeper.

If John didn't like your call, he would hang up right away. But almost every time he picked up on me, he liked my call and I got through. John would tell me to hold on and Howard picked up real quick. That meant John put my name and topic near the top of Howard's list on his computer screen.

I would call in as a character Larry, based on a mailman who drank and hung out at Mr. Beery's bar all the time. I imitated Larry's whiny voice and made him a chronic masturbator working at the post office, jerking off on everyone's mail. When Larry saw me at the bar, he'd say, "Joey, you gotta stop doing me on the Stern Show. People at work really think its me." I thought that was pretty fucking funny and that just made me want to do it more.

So I just started calling in and getting through more often, asking questions and messing with celebrities. Like that time I fucked with Roseanne Barr.

Back when I was a volunteer firefighter on Long Island, the cops used to hang out in the back room with us. So we'd be privy to a lot of inside information about what was going on in neighboring towns.

So one weekend, Roseanne Barr and Meryl Streep were in town filming the movie *She Devil* in the village of Belmar. They were shooting scenes at a pink mansion at the end of Cliff Road.

Word got around town that Roseanne was staying at Danfords Inn, a really nice waterfront hotel in Port Jefferson. So one night, the cops told us they got called to the hotel. When they arrived, Roseanne was drunk out of her mind cursing and screaming and throwing patio furniture off the second floor balcony. The cops went up, calmed her down and brought her back in her room. There was no police report and no one ever found out about it.

So when Roseanne was a guest on the Stern Show, I called in and said, "Howard, listen I was a security guard working on the set of *She-Devil*. Remember that cute little white dog in the movie? Well on the set, that dog pulled off Roseanne's scarf and she went up and kicked it like a football. She broke the dog's damn ribs and they had to get another dog to replace it in the movie."

Howard said, "Roseanne, what the hell?"

She said, "I didn't do that."

I said, "Don't even lie about it Roseanne. Howard, later on that night she got so drunk. She was staying at Danfords Inn down in Port Jefferson. She got so drunk, she was up on the 2nd floor balcony throwing patio furniture off, screaming and cussing. The cops had to come and they put her back in her room and they never wrote it up. They kept it under wraps, but Howard I swear all this is true."

Howard said, "I believe you. And Roseanne, I can't believe you kicked a dog."

She's like, "I didn't," but sounded really shocked when I said the thing about the balcony. "Who are you?"

"I was working security for the movie."

Because half of what I said was a BS lie but the other half was the truth, that kind of fucked her head up a little bit and I could hear it in her voice. It was just pretty funny I did that to her.

I just kept calling up Howard and did a bunch of other pranks to people. Goofy phone calls that were funny and that they seemed to like. Then I built up confidence and told Stuttering John who I was. I was like, "Hey John. My name is really Joe Bootsolino. I do this and this all the time."

John said he recognized my voice and that he went to high school with my brother Vinnie back in Massapequa. I was like yeah you were two years ahead of me. We knew a lot of the same people. Dr. Petrakis, the head of the social studies department whose life I tried to save, had been John's history teacher.

I told him I was using the name Joey Boots now. He said, "Yeah, I'll just keep putting you on cause you got some good calls." And after that, John knew who I was.

As the Stern Show ended for the day, I would move the dial over to the Radio Chick Show on WNEW-FM. That station just switched from a rock music format to talk shows and Leslie Gold aka the Radio Chick was one of their first hosts.

Compared to all the redialing I had to do to get on Howard, I was able to get on the Radio Chick Show easily.

And I always made them laugh really hard cause their shit was lame. I emailed Leslie and told her I'd call up Howard the next day and work her name in.

So I called and said, "Howard, was that you I saw at a dinner table with Leslie Gold the Radio Chick from WNEW the other night?"

Howard said, "No, which is not to say I wouldn't."

"I thought it was you and I got pictures of the both of you and I'm gonna sell them."

The Radio Chick emailed me that day really excited, thanking me and saying to keep doing that. I think I made one more Leslie Gold call to Howard.

I started sending tapes, jokes and ideas into the Radio Chick Show. Never for any money but just for the fun and pride of contributing to something that was reaching thousands of people.

And I wound up being a guest on her show. They had this "Stupid Wheel" they spun to see what stunt you had to do. They wound up piercing my ear. I thought it was a lame bit that sucked for radio, because the listeners at home couldn't even see it. So I spiced it up by pretending to be really scared and in severe pain when I got pierced. I screamed like an animal when they did it. The joke was on me though cause it did actually hurt. Ow!

Buddy Bolton was the Radio Chick's producer. He was very edgy and funny and couldn't even do most of the things he wanted to do, but he did some funny shit. With each of my bits that got on the radio, Buddy said he would try to get me a position on the show or another job at the station. I was excited about that.

One night, they asked if I would go with a bunch of them to put Radio Chick bras on the statues in Central Park. So at 4 a.m. I went with Buddy and a couple of local comedians into the park with bags full of large bras. We climbed up on statues and put the bras on them.

Later that morning, the whole crew at WNEW was waiting for the media storm and shockwave to erupt about the bras. But that never happened. No one seemed to notice or care about the stunt. So they had someone from their own station call in and pretend to be a listener who was in the park. The caller said, "OMG, somebody threw Radio Chick bras on all the statues in Central Park!"

But even then no other news outlets bit on the story. The only person I heard talking about it that day was the Radio Chick. She said, "It must be secret fans of mine that are trying to promote me. That's great!"

Like I said, that show was pretty lame.

CHAPTER 14

FUCKING LISA LAMPANELLI

One of the frequent guests on the Radio Chick was Lisa Lampanelli. She was good friends with producer Buddy Bolton. Lisa later became a well-known comedienne with her standup and roasts, but was just starting out back then.

One night, I went out with Lisa and Buddy to the New York Comedy Club in the east 20s. They both did a standup set there that night. Then we went out for drinks. Buddy had to leave while Lisa and I had more drinks and talked a couple more hours. I walked Lisa back to her friend's apartment where she was staying. Before parting I asked for her number.

I called her a couple days later to see if she wanted to get more drinks and hang out. She invited me to her comedy show that night and said we could do something after.

So I went to her show. Lisa looked the same back then and was funny as hell in the club. No, she wasn't a Playboy centerfold, but I liked her personality, humor and confidence. That's what I was attracted to. Like she was really cool. And fucking hilarious man. She was doing the insult comedy and racial humor and had the whole place including me dying.

After Lisa's set, we went out for dinner and drinks at a restaurant by the river. Then we went back to her friend's place. On the elevator ride up, she said her friend wouldn't be home that night. I thought, "Okay, I'm not a super genius but that sounded like a hint."

As soon as we got in and closed the door we began fucking around, kissing right away. I started making out crazy with her, biting her, nibbling her. We stopped and took off all of our clothes.

How did she look naked? She was a mess. But so was I dude. Fat and out of shape you know, but whatever. It was fine. I just dove right in, eating her pussy. Then I took my cock, stuck it in her mouth, pulled it out, and smacked her in the face with it. She's like, "Yeah hit me with it, hit me with it!"

I kept smacking her face with my cock. She's like, "Pull my hair, pull my hair," and I started pulling her hair. "Squirt it in my face. Squirt it all over my fucking face." You know?

So I fucking jack off in her face. We took a little break, cuddling.

Then we got to some deep hard fucking. I didn't tell her at the time, but I took a Viagra pill before. Because of this, I was hard as a rock and came so fucking fast.

But since I was wearing a condom, Lisa didn't know that I'd already cum. So I just kept fucking through the second fuck. And by the time I nutted for the second time, she thought it was the first time. I've used this move a lot with girls and guys and recommend it to all my bros out there. You'll come off looking like a stallion like I did that night.

Lisa's like, "You fucking stud," and I'm like, "Yeah yeah yeah!"

Another night, we left the city together in a Town Car. We went to a Hilton in New Jersey down by the Meadowlands. We brought a bottle of champagne with us and had another night of dirty, dirty sex. It was just really good.

We never talked about going out or being boyfriend and girlfriend. It just petered out and the next thing I knew she was dating some black guy.

She was a good girl.

CHAPTER 15

PORNOWEEN

I got bored with the Radio Chick and tired of waiting for a job from them. Buddy Bolton kept saying it would happen soon, and all I had to do was prove myself with more contributions to the show.

It started feeling like a lot of work for no gain considering they had so few listeners. When I called the Howard Stern Show, even if it was just for a few seconds, people in my life would contact me saying they were excited to hear my voice. But not one person ever said, "Hey Joey, I loved what you did on the Radio Chick today."

So I decided to concentrate my phone calling energy exclusively on the Howard Stern Show. Even if it took longer to get on the air, why waste time with bland alternatives? My ultimate goal was to first be invited to visit Howard's studio at the K-Rock radio station. Then start contributing more to the show and ultimately land a permanent gig. I thought of my Radio Chick experience as practice for something bigger. And the Howard Stern Show was the biggest radio show in the country.

A few days before Halloween in 2000, Howard announced a contest called Pornoween. They were gonna hide porn star Leanna Heart somewhere in Manhattan. Howard would give clues about her whereabouts and the listener who found her first would win a date and the chance to bang Leanna. They couldn't legally promise sex as a prize because that would violate New York prostitution laws, but it was more than implied.

The first listener who found Leanna needed to put their hand on her shoulder and say, "Woochie woochie, give me your coochie."

So I was all psyched and wanted to do this contest and win. I wanted to get this porn star in bed, and also jumped at the chance to get more involved with the show.

During those years, the E! Entertainment cable channel aired highlights of the Stern Show. So Howard asked if any listeners participating in the contest would be willing to have TV cameras follow them around as they searched for Leanna. I called in and volunteered. So on Halloween morning, a producer and cameraman came to my apartment in Bethpage, went in my car and filmed me driving into the city.

I had to think of where to park while waiting for the first clues. I decided to start around the East 50s near the

K-Rock studio. I figured they would want to bring Leanna and whoever won back to the studio quickly for an interview after the contest. So I parked and waited.

At 6 a.m. Howard came on the radio and his first words were, "You can find implants here."

Implants? And I'm like fuck - Scores! The most obvious fucking place! Scores was the strip club they were always talking about and hanging out at back then.

I was like what fucking street is that on again? Is it on 60th or 61st? I didn't know so I started driving that way. Then I called my friend who gave me the address and I was off. I jetted to Scores and saw the marquee.

The porno pussy was mine! There was no way anyone could have figured out that clue and gotten there before me. And I was the first... besides this other guy! Yup, right as I arrived I saw another dude running into Scores just a few feet ahead.

He approached Leanna, put his hand on her shoulder and yelled, "Woochie woochie, give me the hoochie!" So he actually said the phrase wrong! It was supposed to be, "Woochie woochie, give me your coochie."

But even still, they declared this guy Seth the winner. And I'm like fuck that. He's not the winner you know? And I just sat there on the Scores stoop dejected, watching them walk out together. Leanna and Seth got in the limo and went to the studio for an interview. That should have been me.

I was pissed off man. So I called the show on my way home. Howard put me on the air and I said, "This is fucked up. The guy didn't even say the phrase right. He should have been disqualified immediately." Robin Quivers started laughing and howling at me, saying things like, "Ha ha you're a loser." They laughed, mocked me a little more then hung up.

It turned out the winner Seth was from a very well-off family. They were pissed when they heard him on the radio. His family threatened to cut him off financially if he went on the date with Leanna or did anything else involving the Stern Show again. So a couple days later, he backed out and canceled the date.

So I was like fuck this man. I called in right away. Stuttering John picked up and I said, "John, its Joey Boots. Put me on. I'm the runner-up man. I'll fuck Leanna Heart."

He put me on the air with Howard and I repeated my demands, but said "bang" instead of "fuck." You couldn't curse on the show back then.

"This guy doesn't want to bang her? I'll step in and do the deed," I said.

After acknowledging my status as the runner-up, Howard asked, "Leanna Heart, will you bang Joey Boots?"

"Sure, I'll bang Joey Boots!"

I shouted, "Yeah yeah yeah! Say it again!" She repeated it a few times and Howard congratulated me. And that was the first time my name was repeated multiple times by different people on the show. It was an enthralling moment for me.

A few days later it was time for my big date. They put us in the penthouse suite of the Helmsley Hotel in a fancy room overlooking Central Park. When I got there I found Leanna, her mom Deb and an E! TV cameraman waiting for me in the room. Leanna's mom was always with her and even cleaned cum off of her after filming porno sex scenes.

Before they left us, the guy from the E! channel asked if he could leave the video camera in there and point it away from the bed. That way they could catch audio from our encounter without violating our sexual privacy. We said sure.

When we were alone, I took out a bottle of champagne and tried to set the mood. But Leanna said she didn't drink. So we just took off our clothes and got right to it. I took off my shirt and she began stripping.

Just like when I fucked Lisa Lampanelli, before I got there I took a Viagra and put on a rubber for sex. The last thing I wanted was to be a two-pump wonder. Cum real quick and then I'm known on the Stern Show for that.

So I was fucking her and on the third or fourth pump, I nutted in the rubber. But I didn't say nothing. I just kept fucking and then fucked for another 10-11 minutes. Then I wanted to fuck again.

I pulled off my pants, bent her over the side of the bed and put her on all fours. Then I stood up on the side of the bed and fucked her doggiestyle from behind standing up. I had more control that way and could reach around and play with her titties, pull her hair and choke her. She wanted to be choked.

Then I remembered the camera audio was recording. I wanted to get a good sound bite they could play on the Stern Show and give this moment some legs. So while I was fucking her, I started smacking Leanna's ass and told her to shout "F Jackie!" That was to Jackie "the Jokeman" Martling, the Stern Show writer and sidekick at the time. So I smacked her ass and she shouted, "F Jackie, F Jackie!" I'm like, "Say it again bitch," and she shouted it again loud. Then the next couple of days, Howard played that clip repeatedly. Cool.

The next morning, I visited the Stern Show to talk about what happened on my Pornoween date. That was my first time in the studio. I was a little nervous but not much. I was like wow. I'm finally here in front of the man. Looking around I saw Robin, Jackie, Fred Norris and everyone who I'd been listening to for years. All the people who made the show great and funny. But it also felt very normal and natural, like a group of friends just talking and laughing.

They asked for all the details. Howard was still on censored terrestrial radio so I couldn't get too graphic. We did a whole interview. Leanna called in and said I was real good in bed.

And that made me look good.

CHAPTER 16

MAN IN THE SKY

A lot of Howard Stern fans call into the show or win contests and that's the last you hear from them. But I had
some staying power. After Pornoween, I just kept calling
and throwing ideas at them. Sending in song parody ideas
and making up games.

Like remember Terri Schiavo? She was the Florida lady
in a coma, and her husband wanted to pull the plug but her
family went to court to keep her alive. So I made up the "Terri
Schiavo Game" where I played sounds she was making and
sounds of a humpback whale. People had to guess which
sound was which. Howard played the game twice that day.

I was also able to use my access to the show as a way of
connecting with interesting people. Like have you ever met
a man who could fly? I have.

In October 2000, an Australian author named Brett de
la Mare flew around NYC. He took off from Liberty State
Park in New Jersey using a paraglider he constructed in

Australia. It was a parachute with a powerful fan strapped to his back that kept him in the air.

He flew around the Statue of Liberty, then around the Twin Towers. When he was flying over the World Trade Center, he began throwing flyers down to the street. The flyers said that he was looking for a publisher for a book that he just wrote.

Soon there were cops on the ground and police helicopters overhead. He flew up the East Side past the United Nations and hovered over a pro-Palestinian demonstration. He threw more book flyers on that crowd. Then circled the Empire State Building. He flew up to Harlem then back down to Central Park, throwing flyers and being tailed by helicopters.

When he was over Central Park, the fucking fan stopped and gave out right over the Jackie Onassis Reservoir. He was like fuck and knew he had to land quickly because now he was coming down heavy with this big fan on his back. He saw an opening and crash-landed into a dumpster of the NYPD precinct in the park. Brett looked up and was surrounded by cops.

So they arrested his ass and charged him with reckless endangerment. I watched him on the news that night being taken away in cuffs. As he passed the cameras he shouted, "My name is Brett de la Mare," and gave his email. It was very faint but I heard it. So I typed up an email to him right away. I was like, "Dude, wanna be famous? I'll get you on Howard Stern tomorrow morning. Call me any time. Here's my number."

Within a few hours he bailed himself out for $100. The cops also confiscated his paraglider. After reading my email, Brett called me and I was like, "Dude, I'll get you on the Howard Stern Show. Just meet me tomorrow morning."

So the next morning, we met outside the K-Rock building. KC Armstrong and Gary Dell'Abate, Howard's producers, came out to the lobby and I told them who he was. They took us up to the green room and then he went on the show. Howard made the best of it, but Brett was real nervous man. I didn't think he gave a great interview. Only lasted about 15 minutes before Howard wrapped it up. But I got him on the show.

The judge gave Brett a light sentence of two weeks community service for his antics, cleaning up garbage by the 72nd street boat yard. When he finished that, he got his paraglider back. We put it in my truck and took it out to Long Island where I had a couple friends try to fix the throttle, which had been fucked up when he crashed.

Then we started making plans to do another flying stunt, this time during the "Subway Series" - Mets vs. Yankees World Series in 2000. We went and scoped out Yankee and Shea Stadium for nearby parks with good aerial approaches. The plan was for him to fly in and land on the field with a giant "Baba Booey" banner. That was the nickname of Stern producer Gary Dell'Abate and a code word for any fan that wants to disrupt live broadcasts. So doing this on live TV in front of millions of viewers would be epic.

The closest parks we found were Van Cortlandt Park in the Bronx and Corona Park by Shea. A police officer in Corona asked what we were doing. I said, "We're thinking of dropping in on the World Series." The cop said, "That's a good idea, but tickets are expensive."

So the first night of the World Series, we were in Van Cortlandt Park. I called Doug Goodstein, the producer of Howard's E! channel show, and told him about our plan, and to look for a guy flying in with a "Baba Booey" banner. Doug and other people from the show were at the game that night, so they were all excited.

But there wasn't enough wind for Brett to fly in that night. The second night we had enough wind, but his fucking throttle got stuck again. He could run with it but wouldn't take off. It was too dangerous. So we had to abandon it.

We tried to fix it again, this time in Queens. But every night we failed for one reason or another. Either a mechanical malfunction or not enough wind. So we never fucking did it and Brett just started getting depressed.

I said, "You know what you should do? I think you should go to England and fly into Buckingham Palace with a giant 'Baba Booey' banner. Get your friends stationed along your route and videotape it. Then you can sell it to news organizations and promote yourself."

And that happened. Brett flew in and landed in the full court of Buckingham Palace with the banner. Soon as he landed he got stomped on by the fucking guards there and dragged into the basement by British military intelligence. They interrogated Brett, asking who Baba Booey was. But his friends fucked up. They were total amateurs and didn't get all the good footage or get it out to the media. In the prank world, if a tree falls and no one recorded it, it never happened. Then you might just get in trouble without the publicity payoff.

I heard Brett went back to Australia. He never flew into my life again.

CHAPTER 17

THE ART OF THE BOOEY BOMB

Like I said before, one thing Howard Stern fans love doing is pranking and disrupting live shows by shouting Stern Show jokes and references. We shout things like "Baba Booey," "Howard Stern Rules," "Howard Stern's Penis," and other phrases related to the show. Targets of these pranks include reporters, C-SPAN call-in segments and quiet golf broadcasts. These fan interruptions are called "Booey Bombs." And I mastered the art.

If you walk around NYC enough, you see reporters filming live news stories. You go behind them in the middle of a report, yell "Baba Booey!" and screw their shit up. Sometimes they laugh and roll with it, but usually they get real annoyed. Either a producer or security will usher you away or they'll cut back to the studio.

I have a very loud deep voice, which makes me more effective than the average. Not only is it fun, but what's also cool about it is Howard will play these pranks on the show. If it's particularly funny or disruptive, you'll become part of the rotation of bumpers - when they go in and out of commercial breaks.

Some of my prankings and spankings on the news got a bit more elaborate than doing a simple Booey Bomb. Here are a couple of my favorite efforts.

I was home watching CNN Sunday February 18, 2001. That day, legendary NASCAR driver Dale Earnhardt was killed in a fatal car crash in Florida at the Daytona 500. I never followed car racing or heard of him before, but his fans were understandably devastated. CNN was covering the tragedy all day. Now they ran a piece about Dale Earnhardt's stomach cancer charity.

Then I thought you know what? Let me try to do a prank. So I called CNN. They picked up, and I told the operator I was Dale Earnhardt's cousin. Without asking any more questions, they put me through live on CNN.

I got on the air and said to the newswoman, "Yeah, I just wanted to correct you on one of those stories. Dale didn't just donate to stomach cancer. He donated to all different types of cancer research."

The newswoman asked how I knew this. I said I was his cousin KC Armstrong from Long Island.

"Really?"

"Yeah," I said.

The fake name I used - KC Armstrong - was one of the Howard Stern Show producers. But it wasn't as obvious a prank as shouting "Baba Booey," so CNN was still going along with me.

The newswoman gave me her condolences. I said how it was a rough time for our family and there was gonna be a memorial service that weekend on Long Island. She said she was sorry for my loss then asked if I could hang on and talk to one of their producers off air.

I started getting a little nervous as they treated me more serious. I thought the prank would be over by now. So when the producer got on the phone, I said I wasn't looking for attention and started to hang up. The producer said she understood, but Dale Earnhardt meant so much to the country. And they would really like if someone from the family could come on the air for an interview at 6 a.m. the next morning.

I figured I'd see where this went.

The producer asked me questions about Dale. I said, "Yeah, he was not only my cousin but my best friend. I always talked to him whenever he was here in New York. He'd visit me on Long Island." I said this was why we were having a memorial service here because he spent so much time with us. The producer said, "Beautiful," and confirmed my 6 a.m. interview.

This blew my mind. I never thought it would go this far. I was still convinced they would do some fact checking and not even call. That night I went to Mr. Beery's bar across the street and got real drunk thinking about it. Two guys at the bar wanted to drink with me all night then come to my place and wait for the call.

So at 5:30 the next morning I was sitting by my phone with these two guys. Sure enough, at 5:50 the phone rang and it was CNN. The producer asked if I was ready for the interview. "We'll be running this as the top news story then cut to you on the phone."

I said, "Yeah, no problem."

My friends were sitting there on the couch amazed and already cracking up. I gave them pillows to put over their mouths and muffle their laughs so they wouldn't make noise and ruin my prank. The reason why most people suck at prank calls is because they can't control their laughter.

At 6 a.m. CNN showed a montage of clips and images from Dale Earnhardt's career. They did a report from Daytona, one from his hometown, then went back to the studio. The anchorwoman Fredricka then said, "On the phone we have Dale Earnhardt's cousin KC Armstrong on Long Island."

"KC, can you hear me?" Fredricka asked.

I said, "Yes Fredricka. I can hear you." I continued, "I just wanted to say my family and I - we're very upset right now. We saw the accident yesterday live on TV and we're just as devastated as the rest of the country. We loved our Uncle Dale and he meant so much to us."

"I'm sure he did. What did Dale Earnhardt mean to you personally?"

I got teary and said, "He was my best friend you know? Whenever I had problems, I would go to him and we could talk about anything. He was my best friend and I'm gonna miss him."

"Oh, I totally understand," Fredericka said.

I wailed, "I'm sorry I'm all emotional at a time like this."

She kept saying she understood. I was thinking to myself NASCAR fans across the country watching this are probably in tears right now.

Then I'm like, "I just wanna say that today on Long Island, we are having a memorial service for my Uncle Dale. It will be presided by Reverends Benjy Bronk and John Melendez." Those were more names of people who worked on the Stern Show.

"Both reverends will be at the church tomorrow," I continued. "And… I just want to say that… Howard Stern is the greatest!"

And then Fredericka's like, "Oh oh oh oh!" They hung up and Fredricka's like, "I am so sorry. Usually we check very hard, but this one just seemed to get through. I deeply apologize." They cut right to another segment.

Dude, do you know how many death threats I got after that prank aired on Stern? I got death threats in my emails from hardcore Dale Earnhardt fans all over the world. And when I put my video of the prank up on YouTube, his fans left nasty fucking messages on my channel. Pretty fucking cruel stuff. But that was a great prank phone call though.

*   *   *

It was the first Independence Day since the 9/11 terrorist attacks. On July 4th, 2002, the nation was still shaken and Homeland Security was on high alert.

That day, a gunman opened fire at the El Al Israeli Airlines ticket counter at Los Angeles Airport. Three people were killed before police shot and killed the guy. It turned out the attacker was an Egyptian taxi driver, but nobody knew that at the time.

I was watching this unfold live on CNN. Then I got the idea to try another prank on them. So I called up CNN and again got through to an operator right away. I said I was at the airport and trying to get ahold of my wife to let her know I was okay.

They said, "Wait, you're at the airport?"

"Yes, I was at the ticket counter when the shooting happened."

They said, "Listen, will you go on the air? Then your family will be able to hear you and know you're safe."

They asked my name and I said, "Yosef Bootski." I wanted my name to sound Israeli - like the type of guy who would be getting on an El Al flight.

So they put me on the air and interviewed me. I told them my wife and I had just gotten our tickets at the counter. We were walking towards the gate when we suddenly heard shooting.

The reporter asked if I saw who was responsible for the shots. I said that I turned around and saw a gunman with blond hair in a ponytail shooting. And the guy was yelling, "Artie took my job! Artie took my job!" over and over again.

I described the gunman as looking like Jackie the Jokeman, the Stern Show writer who just quit the show. Comedian Artie Lange had just taken his place.

On this call with CNN, I didn't shout out "Howard Stern Rules" or "Baba Booey." That was the end and CNN moved on.

But then that day on Israeli Prime Minister Benjamin Netanyahu's website, there was an article with the fake information I had just given. My account of what happened made international newspapers across the globe. They picked up the story and quoted Yosef Bootski.

And later I was watching a news conference on MSNBC with the deputy director of the FBI. One reporter asked, "Is it true the gunman was yelling 'Artie took my job?'"

"We don't know yet. We're still looking into that," the FBI director replied.

It was hilarious. This was ten hours later and a lot of people still hadn't figured it out.

I understand most people think its wrong to make jokes and exploit emergency moments like this.

But doing these types of pranks excited me. It was the same rush I got from doing pranks as a teenager. Fucking with people in funny, but kind of fucked up ways. But whereas in the past I was doing it completely anonymously, now it was helping me gain more notoriety and delve deeper into the Howard Stern universe.

CHAPTER 18

ICY HOT WACKNESS

S ome of my Howard Stern Show memories probably sound obscure to all but the most hardcore fans. But they're precious moments to me.

One of my best memories was on Howard's last day on terrestrial FM radio, as he was moving to uncensored Sirius Satellite Radio. This was December 2005. He was up on the stage on 56th street between 5th and 6th Ave with the whole area packed with thousands of fans. During Howard's "Last of a Dying Breed" speech, he spotted me in the crowd, mentioned my name and gave me special thanks. That was a really proud moment.

For a little while, I owned the website address for OpieandAnthony.com. Opie and Anthony were a New York radio team who were always trying to start a verbal war with Howard, whereas Howard barely even knew who they were and never took the bait. O&A did attract the scorn of fans like me though. Anthony Comia forgot to make a payment and renew the website address. So I took over their site and redirected it to Hank the Angry Drunken Dwarf's homepage.

Hank the Angry Drunken Dwarf? Well, he was an angry drunken dwarf. They found him stumbling outside the K-Rock radio station building. He came up to the show, talked about his drunken life and even pulled down his pants to show Howard what a little person's penis looked like. A star was born.

Hank quickly became a beloved member of the Stern Show Wack Pack. The Wack Pack is an assortment of retards, lame brains, stutterers and basically anyone associated with the show who stays consistently wacky. Hank the Dwarf got so popular that in 1998 he won the *People Magazine* online poll for the "Most Beautiful Person" as a write-in candidate. He beat out Brad Pitt and Leonardo DiCaprio for the title. But *People Magazine* made up some dumb reason to disqualify the little guy. I think today they would be accused of dwarf discrimination.

Hank was a real funny guy and I became friends with him. That's why I redirected Opie and Anthony's site to his homepage. CBS, who owned their show, went all the way to the World Intellectual Property Organization to take the site back from me. I tried finding a pro bono lawyer to take my case on First Amendment grounds. Then I tried to sell the website back to CBS. But they weren't looking to buy. They were looking to take it back from me, which they did because

I had no money to pay for a lawyer. O&A's producer later told me I cost their legal department $10,000. So I lost the battle and the war, but got to annoy rich people for a little while.

Then there was the Icy Hot stunt.

A few listeners and I went up to the K-Rock studio on Halloween wearing costumes related to the Stern Show. I dressed up as "Cokie Lange," because Artie Lange had bad drug problems in those years. For my costume, I had on a sweatshirt with white powder all over my shirt and face. And I went in and did that smoky, wheezy Artie cough-laugh for my impression.

That day, Johnny Knoxville from the *Jackass* TV stunt show was visiting, promoting the first *Jackass* movie. Howard was inspired to make his own version of *Jackass* called *Jerkoff*. So Howard had me and the other costumed listeners go out on the street and find someone to perform a *Jerkoff* stunt involving High Pitch Eric. Eric is a plus-size Wack Packer known for his high speaking voice and willingness to do anything Howard and co. could suggest, usually in a thong.

We needed to find someone willing to have High Pitch Eric shave off their pubes, then glue the hairs to their face, forming a mustache. Then Eric would spread Icy Hot ointment on your freshly shaved mound. The prize for doing this was an all-expense-paid trip to Hong Kong.

We went on the streets and tried to find someone. But no one wanted to do it. Not even homeless people. I was in the green room as Howard was about to give up on the stunt. Just then I stepped up and volunteered. A free trip to Hong Kong and more radio airtime seemed like a good deal. I also thought it would be something funny to do.

So I went in the studio, took off my pants and pulled down my underwear. They made fun of my small penis because I'm only 6 inches when hard, and the studio was really cold - shrinkage! Plus when you're on the husky side you tend to look even smaller from that. The shit crawled up inside of me. Howard and them called it a bird in a nest, a button.

I didn't really care about being naked and exposed in the studio. Even though there were cameras recording for the E! show, I knew my crotch would be blurred out and pixilated on TV.

So I laid down on the table. High Pitch clipped off my pubes then glued them to my face with spirit gum and made a mustache. Then he spread Icy Hot ointment on my crotch. It actually didn't even hurt at all. It just felt kind of cool and refreshing. I was like this is no problem. We all laughed, they clapped and said I was a good sport as I left the studio.

But the thing about Icy Hot is it starts out icy then gets hot. They really named that product well. So I was out in the hallway discussing the bit with Dave Grohl and the Foo

Fighters, the next guests on the show. Just then, my crotch started to burn like a motherfucker man. I threw off my headphones and ran down the hall to the staff bathroom. I turned the sink on full blast, pulled down my pants and threw my cock and balls under the faucet. And I just started screaming in pain. The cameras followed me and filmed all this.

When word got to the studio about what I was going through, Howard and Johnny Knoxville ran out to see me and howled with laughter at my predicament. It was pretty funny man. Howard later dug up an extra $2,000 in prize money for my suffering. It was a good half hour before the pain in my balls subsided.

I didn't even end up going on the prize trip to Hong Kong. I sold the vacation back to the sponsor for $3,500. So all in all I made out with $5,500. I gave High Pitch Eric $1,000 because he was becoming a good friend of mine. With the rest I paid some bills and bought some drugs. I bought a lot of drugs back then man.

CHAPTER 19

BEETLE

Some people have asked if I'm part of the Howard Stern Show Wack Pack. While there's no defined rules for being a member of the Pack, I think there needs to be something extreme about your physical appearance, voice or mental health. Yes, I am on the "husky" side, but to me that's not enough. So no I don't think I'm in the Wack Pack. But I did hang out with a few of them.

I used to go out and get high with Beetlejuice, who was like a Wack Pack rock star at one point. Beetle is a little black midget pinhead with messed up teeth. He says the craziest things and Howard always had fun asking him questions and getting bizarre, random responses. He'll give a different age, height and weight for himself each time he's asked.

But the little guy was a superstar, so he used to do a lot of paid fan appearances. I'd sometimes tag along on these gigs with Beetle and his manager Sean Rooney. We'd all show up in a limo and make a big deal out of it. We smoked a lot of crack and sniffed powder on the way to these gigs.

One of these events was in Atlantic City. 10 couples paid $3,500 each to have a steak dinner with Beetle in the back room of a casino steakhouse. They would also get to gamble with him after.

So we were at this steak dinner, and Beetle was at the center of the table drinking booze out of a giant medieval goblet. The fans were taking pictures, video and talking to him.

Then I said to myself, "I gotta make this a memorable event." I brought along a little bottle of Ipecac, a syrupy drug that induces vomiting. Why did I have that in my pocket? Good question.

So I dropped some Ipecac in Beetlejuice's beer. He took a few more sips out of his goblet. Within a minute, he was projectile vomiting across the table just as these people were finishing up their dinner.

They all jumped up screaming. Waitresses, waiters and cooks came running out of the kitchen. It was loud, frantic chaos and there was just vomit flying everywhere. And Sean, Beetlejuice's manager, wasn't even trying to help. He just kept the video camera rolling, recording the whole thing.

It was really really funny. But dangerous. Don't try that at home kids.

Another great time with Beetlejuice was when we scammed the Judge Mathis TV court show with the help of our friend Drunken Jamie.

Beetle and another midget Dominic used to do these "Dwarf Tossing" events at bachelor parties. They would dress up in superhero costumes and wasted idiots would throw them onto mats. Pretty demeaning, but they made some good money from those parties. I think that's illegal now.

So we contacted *The Judge Mathis Show* and made up a fake case about dwarf tossing. Beetle, Dominic and Sean accused Jamie and me of purposely throwing them off a mat into a wall during a bachelor party. They sued us for $5,000 in lost wages, the maximum amount allowed for a case. The plan was for us to split the money after Beetle's team won. Those shows always cover the damages anyway. And even if we lost, we would be on TV.

So we called in with that case and within a couple of days the show got in touch, wanting to bring us all to Chicago and arbitrate in their TV court.

The night before leaving, we made a video to use as evidence for the show. Sean brought over neighbors to simulate a bachelor party in his garage. Dominic the Dwarf put on a helmet and Superman cape.

Drunken Jamie lifted Dominic up by his costume. I shouted to Jamie, "Throw him off the mat," loud enough so the camera could hear. The whole video was so contrived and horrible. It took us 3 takes for Jamie to throw Dominic into the wall headfirst. We wanted it to look as authentic as possible. Ironically by the 3rd take, Dominic actually was in a lot of pain and probably could have really sued and used that fake evidence as real evidence.

The Judge Mathis Show paid both sides $500 just for appearing. They also provided airfare to Chicago, hotel accommodations and limos.

The case was such a fiasco and slam-dunk in favor of the midgets - especially with that ridiculous video. Judge Mathis asked us to describe dwarf tossing and was appalled that this type of activity existed. He was mad that we brought such shame to his TV court. Mathis awarded Beetle and co. $5,000 and said, "You all get back to Howard. Please leave on the first train moving from Chicago!"

So it was just a goof. And we made a little money and got some attention from Howard, who played clips of our case on the show.

Another time I found myself in a run down warehouse in Jersey City with Beetlejuice. We were in that warehouse for about 10 hours straight man while this local rock band practiced. We had just gotten back from another Beetle fan appearance in Atlantic City. As soon as we got to Jersey City, we bought some crack. Beetle knew just where to get it. We pulled up to a spot in our limo. He ran out, went into a store and came out with a paper bag full of crack stems and brillo. Then we rolled on, stopped on the next block and bought a bunch of crack. We had a lot of money from these appearances so we bought a lot.

We were just hanging out in that warehouse all night. While everyone was in the main room listening to that local band practice, Beetle and I were in the back room smoking crack for 10 hours. I was sitting at a little kiddie table while Beet was next to me, pacing back and forth, running his mouth nonstop about the craziest insane shit. Things he'd done and crimes he committed. I don't believe any of it was true, but it was funny.

Beetle.

CHAPTER 20

GATES OF HELL

A week before the 9/11 terrorist attacks, the Stern Show suffered its own profound tragedy. We lost Hank the Dwarf. He was a great guest on the show and a good friend of mine.

Hank had been partying all weekend down in the Hamptons. Then he went home to his family's house in Fall River, Massachusetts, went to bed and never woke up.

High Pitch Eric and I started a memorial for Hank on the sidewalk outside of the K-Rock studio. For three days and nights, thousands of people came by and left mementos. Be it flowers or pictures, bongs, weed, booze. A lot of people came by and it was really beautiful man. And every morning Howard would broadcast from the sidewalk out there.

Then I went to Hank's wake and funeral. I took a van up to Fall River with High Pitch Eric and a bunch of people from the Howard E! show. Richie Wilson, Mike Gange and Doug Goodstein, who had also been acting as Hank's manager. In fact, Doug had just recently offered me a job to drive and escort Hank to some of the paid fan appearances he was doing.

I went to say goodbye to Hank at his open casket. It was so sad man. To see somebody who was so vibrant and full of life lying motionless. It was sad. I put a little vodka bottle in his jacket. I still miss him. He really was a beautiful person.

Soon after that, the world would change forever man.

We got back to New York from Hank's funeral. I went to my apartment in Bethpage to shower and grab some clothes. Still feeling emotional and not wanting to be alone, I came into the city and stayed with a gay friend for the weekend. We partied, went out to clubs, did some coke and had a little casual sex. Just a friend - a fuck buddy. I don't want to say his name because he's still on the radio in NY and not out about his sexuality. It wasn't Opie or Anthony though.

My friend lived over on West 4th street and 7th Ave. So we were just coming back from a club and it was early in the morning on Tuesday, September 11th 2001.

Just then, we heard a sudden and very loud banging noise. We thought it was coming from the apartment next door. Then we heard a woman screaming. Doors slamming. Then the sounds of a lady screaming and bolting down the hallway, running outside. We ran out to follow her into the street and see what the fuck she was doing, what was going on, and if she needed help. We saw her run up to the corner of this West Village block. We still thought it was just this one lady bugging out. But when we reached the corner, we looked down 7th Avenue and very prominently in front of us were the Twin Towers. And one of them was smoking like crazy.

And we were like what the fuck man you know? Then we heard a plane crashed into it. We were just standing there, watching in disbelief. Like most people around the country, at that moment we thought it was just a horribly tragic accident.

My next instinct was to call Howard Stern, who was live that morning. Stuttering John picked up my call and put me on hold. While I was on hold, a second plane approached from the south and slammed into the second tower.

And it was just totally deliberate you know? Wow our whole world changed after that man. And I was very angry and emotional by the time Howard picked up on me. I was the first call Howard took after the second plane hit and everyone realized it was terrorism. And we were now at war.

I told Howard where I was and what I saw. And I was very emotional and told him how I felt man. I told him who it was - that it was Osama Bin Laden and some dirty towel heads. Why do we have them in our country? We need to throw them out. Immediately I said and knew it was Bin

Laden. Whatever I said at the time I didn't have a filter on anything. It was pure rage and emotion and anger.

On the phone, I said anybody out there right now working in any kind of NYC landmark should be on the lookout, because these guys like to do these things in multiple numbers. "There's more attacks coming," I warned. And there were more attacks coming. But my thinking wasn't broad enough man, cause it wasn't just New York. It was all across the country. It was Flight 93, which went down in Shanksville, Pennsylvania and Northern Virginia at the Pentagon.

It was just really big for me to be on the air, giving live information to millions of people. I felt like I was able to pour my grief out to someone. I just wanted to scream at somebody and tell someone something. And I was able to do that through the Howard Stern Show with people that I loved. It's amazing to look back on it now.

Later on, Howard got a lot of credit for staying on the radio for hours during and after the attack. For so many people that day, the show was an important source for live updates and helped them process what was going on.

I spent that night on Church Street, just up the block from the destroyed Twin Towers. My friend and I sat at a bar called Sugar with the owners and people from the neighborhood, watching emergency vehicles go by. And we just drank, smoked weed outside and watched TV news to make sense of what was happening just a few blocks away.

We looked down the street and saw the smoky remains of the towers. There were pieces of paper from obliterated offices and dust blowing up the street.

Then I got the idea to head up to the Stern Show and try to get on the air that morning. The show started at 6 a.m. The subways weren't running and there wasn't a cab in sight. So at about 3 a.m. I started walking uptown from below Canal Street. I walked all the way up to 57th street, which is quite a distance - about 4 miles. Deserted city man. I'm telling you there was nobody out. It was like the apocalypse happened. I maybe saw a couple of people when I walked through Times Square, but it was so odd to walk in the city with nobody around.

I made it up to 57th street and went up into the K-Rock studio. I slept on the green room couch for the first half of the show.

And for the last hour, Howard had me in to talk about the day before. Everyone who was in New York that day remembers their 9/11 story. And that morning I told mine. But I left out the gay sex and drugs.

CHAPTER 21

EDGE OF GLORY

I kept calling and doing things with the Howard Stern Show. I got to meet lots of people, some semi-famous. Like the night I went out with porn stars Tabitha Stevens and Ron Jeremy. I saw his penis.

Tabitha Stevens and I were friends through the show. I think it was 2005-6. A lot of it's a blur, but I think we met during Howard's week of doing Vegas shows. So she was in New York and invited me to a 4th of July party at her friend's house in Brooklyn. On the phone she said, "I'm gonna bring my friend along. Do you know Ron?" And I'm like, "Ron who?" She said, "Ron Jeremy." I go yeah I know who he is.

So we met up in her midtown Manhattan hotel room. Ron Jeremy came out of the bathroom and was pulling on his pants. I could see his package and cock, and wow it really was huge. Even bigger looking in person. I was thinking I could never take that penis. It was so big.

We went to a house party in Brooklyn. We lit off fireworks and sat around the kitchen all night, just talking about life. You know Ron used to be a special education teacher and worked as a kayak instructor in Queens. He's a good Jewish boy.

We went to a club, got treated VIP. It was nice man. Bottle service, nothing I had to pay for. I wasn't even dressed right – cargo shorts and a Hawaiian shirt - but they let me in because I was with them.

*   *   *

I became close with other people affiliated with the Stern Show, especially Shuli Egar. We met during Howard's Vegas week. I met so many Stern fans that week. Imagine a radio show crossed with a wild tailgate party. That's what those Vegas shows were like. Shuli was working as a comedian out there on the Strip. Since he started calling the show, I was a fan of the funny things he would say. We hung out a lot that week and stayed in touch after.

I would soon compete against Shuli and 9 other guys in a contest called "Get John's Job."

Stuttering John Melendez left the Stern Show to become Jay Leno's announcer on the *The Tonight Show*. Howard ended up being pissed at Leno for going behind his back to hire his staff. He and others also wondered how someone famous for stuttering would be the announcer on a major TV show. Evidently, it didn't work out because John was soon downgraded to a writer on *The Tonight Show*. That's still a good job though.

So they had a contest to "Get John's Job." The winner would become a producer, personality and whatever else John did. It was a dream job for any Stern fan. And for me it was a chance to achieve true success after waiting for my chance outside of things. I knew I wanted this and was honored and excited to be picked as one of the 10 contestants.

My competition was a who's who of the Stern Show auxiliary squad. They were other fans like me who called the show frequently and got the occasional in-studio appearances for contests, stunts and such.

Looking around the room I saw Sal the Stockbroker, Richard Christy, Yucko the Clown, the Reverend Bob Levy, Dan the Song Parody Man, Crazy Cabbie, Chaunce Hayden and John the Stutterer. Don't confuse John the Stutterer with Stuttering John. The former stutters way worse than the latter on the ladder of stuttering.

Each of the applicants would have one week to produce the show. After everyone had their chance, listeners would call in and vote for the winner. It was a big deal.

One part of the contest was that we each had to get an impressive guest to appear on the show. I asked the bartenders and patrons at Mr. Beery's bar if they knew any freaks in town I could impress Howard with. They all suggested this insane 9/11 widow named Eleanor who lived in Farmingdale. Her husband worked at Cantor Fitzgerald and died in the Twin Towers. They told me she was a total mess.

So I got Eleanor to come into the studio during my producing week. She came with her boyfriend Eric, who just got kicked off the police force for violence and drugs.

Eleanor was a total train wreck and the complete opposite of other 9/11 families highlighted in the media back then. She collected millions from various victim funds. She told Howard how she kept visiting these charities every day and got at least $3 million so far. She wasted all the money buying Harley motorcycles and went on tons of trips.

Eleanor and Eric talked about how they bought a lot of crack and smoked a lot of crack. Her 18-year-old daughter came in and said the boyfriend would blow crack in her face. Eric took off his shirt and Eleanor got topless. The daughter wasn't fazed, saying she'd seen them have sex before.

Eleanor's sister-in-law called in and berated her. It was pretty wild. Lots of callers were completely horrified and offended that this couple was using 9/11 victim money to get rich and be junkies. Lawyer Dominic Barbara called in and said he would contact Child Protective Services, because Eleanor said she had other young children at home.

And when Eleanor got home to Farmingdale, the cops and child services were already there waiting for her to investigate. She told them, "Oh no, that was just for the radio. None of it was true. We made it all up." She had to cover her ass and didn't want her kids taken away.

Howard and Robin said they were two of the best guests ever, and Gary Dell'Abate told me they had an open invitation to come back anytime.

One fan emailed the show saying, "Joey has blown away the competition in nearly every category. That 9/11 widow was the most compelling thing I've heard on this show in months." Another wrote, "Excellent. Joey Boots is kicking serious ass." And finally, "Joey Boots hit a homerun in my book with those fucking crackheads."

So I thought I brought in good guests, had a good week producing and therefore had a decent shot at winning.

A few weeks later, all the contestants were invited back to hear who would get the job. The only one missing was John the Stutterer, who dropped out after barely lasting a day with listeners harassing him on the phone line.

Sal the Stockbroker kept farting and clearing the room. Chaunce showed up in a dress and sandals. At first there was a light-hearted spirit, but as it got closer to hearing who won, it got pretty tense man. Chaunce started crying. Crazy Cabbie and I got in a heated argument.

They went around the studio and the major players on the show said who they thought should win. Howard, Robin and Fred were most impressed with Sal. Gary liked Richard Christy. No one chose me. But I still had hope, since the winner would be chosen based on listeners calling in and voting.

After all the fan votes, Howard made it like *American Idol* and divided the applicants into groups of 3. Each group had one finalist and the other two were eliminated. I was put with Yucko the Clown and Crazy Cabbie. And the finalist among us was… Yucko. I came in 9th place with only 2.8% of the vote, with Shuli behind me in 10th.

In dramatic fashion, Howard announced Richard Christy was the overall winner. He won the job plus $25,000 from contest sponsor TrimSpa. Most in the studio were surprised, because it seemed like Sal the Stockbroker was the favorite.

Well Howard did eventually hire Sal as a writer too. And even Shuli, who came in behind me in the contest, was later brought on as a reporter on the Howard 100 News at Sirius.

And then there was me, in the same place again.

CHAPTER 22

MAD SPONSORS

For a long time, I was very jealous and bitter of Richard, Sal and Shuli. They all began in the same place as me – callers and fans of the show. But those guys got picked up for jobs and I was looked over. Denied a seat at the Howard buffet.

But there were still some perks. A couple Stern Show sponsors stepped up to give me some money and limelight.

During one visit to the studio, Howard and the gang noticed and commented about how fat I was getting. It was pretty humiliating, but true, and I couldn't argue. One of their new sponsors called in and said he would help me lose weight and look better. He was selling a pepper spray diet product. You just sprayed this pepper thing up your nose and it was supposed to inhibit your appetite.

Later we spoke more about the deal. The guy said he would pay me $15,000 to use the spray, plus an extra $500 a week if I agreed to set up a webcam in my apartment so people could track my progress in real time. He would also hook me up with a personal trainer and membership to a Gold's Gym on Long Island. I agreed to this deal and said the webcam would be no problem.

So I used the pepper spray. It smelled, well, peppery. And you know what - it did make me eat less. Plus with the webcam running, there was the extra incentive of not wanting to pig out and look like a failure in front of everyone.

I was doing everything. Going to Gold's Gym, eating good and losing weight. The sponsor loved my progress and lots of people were following me on the cam, giving me positive feedback and encouragement. I was even inspiring others to get in shape.

Then I found myself in the last week of my 6-month contract. We were about to discuss renewing my deal and keeping this going. But then suddenly I was like, "Oh screw it. If these people want to see my life, I'll show them my life." So I did an 8 ball of cocaine on the webcam. And I quickly got fired.

I don't know why I did that. Probably because I'm an addict and self-destructive. But even so, I could have gone into the bathroom to do drugs and no one would have known. Instead I did it in front of the world in the dumbest way possible. And I had to ruin this good thing. I'm a voyeur man. And maybe deep down I want to fuck things up. I was like if I'm gonna do this I'm gonna do something funny. To me that was funny.

So they dropped me. They dropped me the next day. And the story never even got on the Stern Show because then the sponsor would be embarrassed. They just quietly pushed me aside. Familiar territory.

Word got out around the show about my drug problems. I think a lot of people there knew I was going through a lot of stuff. I was personal friends with a few of them like Shuli and Richie Wilson from Howard TV.

During Howard's first year at Sirius Radio, they put me on "Meet the Shrink," a show on the Howard 101 Channel hosted by therapist Dr. Leslie Armstrong. They did an intervention with me on the shrink show. I cried and poured my heart out to Dr. Armstrong about all my problems and drug use. She asked if I would go to rehab if the channel sent me and paid for it. I said most definitely.

So they got me into this rehab in Miami and I was there for 53 days. I did well there and stayed sober. Then I got out and lasted about seven months being clean. Eventually I went out again man. I stopped going to meetings and went out again. But I was still telling everyone that I was living the sober life and found my way. Everyone was proud of me. I was lying to them all.

The Joey Boots healthy revival story was a sham. But it got me another deal from a Stern Show sponsor. This time it was for an alcohol treatment center. They offered $5,000 to record a commercial that would air during the show. I went up to Sirius, went in one of the studios and recorded the commercial maybe twice. And I got paid thousands for just 5 minutes of work. I knew I loved radio.

I was in the throes of my addiction.

So I got $5,000 for that commercial then blew it on coke. I really had no plan, but I had that money and I was like now I'm gonna buy a nice big sack of coke to last me a while. I probably also bought some food, paid my cell bill, maybe paid my rent for the month. I just remember I bought a lot of coke, which I mostly did by myself so no one would find out.

I'd lock myself in my apartment for days, do coke then sit on the internet and harass people. Troll the internet, that's what I did man. A crazy insane life. But also very pathetic and lethargic and full of nothingness. Crazy but nothing happening. Slowly losing my mind and losing myself.

And I called the Stern Show a few weeks later just to make a quick comment about something. I'd been up all night drinking and doing coke, and Howard said, "You sound high man."

"Yeah man, I've been up all night drinking."

"It sounds like you've been doing a little more than drinking."

"Yeah, I just did an 8 ball."

"Where do you get the money to do all this coke, Joey?" Howard asked.

"Oh, you know that rehab commercial airing on your channel? Well they paid me $5,000 and I bought a lot of coke with it."

Robin said, "So you took the money from the alcohol abuse commercial and you bought coke."

That commercial was yanked from the air immediately. Howard laughed and it was a funny joke for the radio that day. But it was pulled. And I was never asked to do another commercial or endorsement.

So again just as things were happening for me, I fucked it up. A lot of shit could have happened. I blew a lot of chances in life. And the money was gone man. Coke's expensive.

CHAPTER 23

COMING OUT

I had several drug relapses and just kept coming back. Then I checked myself into another rehab. There were a bunch of rehabs in there - I think between 2007 and 2009 there were at least five. Four outpatient and one inpatient.

During this time, I decided to come out as a gay guy to the people in my life.

I was trying to get back into programs, trying to get sober again. And I really felt there was this weight, and not just from gaining pounds. I felt if I let it go, somehow it would help me tackle my addiction problems.

I lived my whole life in the closet. I grew up thinking that if anybody found out, then I was gonna have to kill myself. That's how badly I felt about who I was and what I was doing. I feared my family finding out, my friends, everybody. I always felt like there was something wrong with me.

I think the Stern Show and media in general at that time had a lot to do with me getting the courage to come out. I heard and saw people on Howard's show who were openly gay and that nobody thought twice about it. Like Neil Patrick Harris and George Takei. I totally respected them when they came out.

I was just so sick of living a lie man. And I was like you know what? Let me tell my family, let me tell my friends, then let me tell everybody that knows me through the Howard Stern Show.

First I told my mother and father. I sat them down at the dining room table and said, "Listen, I got something really important to talk to you about." I took a deep breath. They were staring intently. I said, "Listen, I'm gay."

At first my parents didn't react. Then my father said that he suspected, and told my mother years ago. And I was like wow. I asked them how they felt about it. They said they just wanted me to be happy. Then they said, "If you're gonna have sex, we want you to have safe sex. We don't want you catching any diseases." I just said thank you so much for being understanding, loving and accepting of me.

I didn't even say the word tolerant. They weren't tolerant of me. They were accepting. Tolerant means I don't agree with that but I'll let it go. But accepting means I accept that's who my son is and I love him.

Next I told my older brother Vinnie and his wife. They were fine with it, cause my sister-in-law – her brother's openly gay. So that was pretty easy. Then I went and told my younger brother Frankie and his wife. And Frankie just started laughing at the dinner table when I told them.

I said, "What are you laughing for?"

He's like, "You're kidding. I know you. You're a jokester. You're playing a game." I'm like, "No Frankie. I'm totally serious."

"Really?"

When he saw I was serious, he said he was fine with it, and that it was okay. He and his wife both said they loved me. My brother even said, "Matter of fact, we have some gay friends that we hang out with all the time and we love them. They're awesome people and we have no problem with that."

So coming out to my family went over way better than I thought it would.

So yeah man then I went on the Howard Stern Show. I wanted it to be a surprise to Howard. But before I went on, I had to first tell Gary Dell'Abate and Will Murray. Gary approves all the Stern guests and Will does the pre-interviews.

I spoke to Gary and said, "Listen, I wanna come in. There's something I wanna talk about. I have a revelation that I want to speak about."

"What is it?" Gary asked.

"This is really hard for me to say. And if it doesn't go through to the show, I want you to keep it to yourself."

Then I told him I was gay. Gary giggled a bit. He goes, "Okay this is good, this is good."

So I told Gary that I lived my whole life in the closet. I felt this was gonna help me in my drug recovery to be honest with others and myself and to live a more free life. To not always be looking over my shoulder, scared that if somebody found out I would have to kill myself. I just wanted to be proud of myself.

And Gary liked all that.

Of course I was nervous man. But I was pretty stalwart with the fact that I was gonna do this. I already did it with my family. And I didn't care what anybody thought.

So then I went on the show and came out. At first, they made it a little game where they had to guess my secret.

"You weren't born a woman?" Howard asked.

I said, "No I still have a penis. I'm gay."

They were really surprised when it was revealed, especially Artie Lange, who refused to believe it. Then I discussed a lot of the gay events of my life like hustling when I was younger, getting raped and discussed my struggles keeping it secret and told some stories. It was very cathartic and emotional for me.

Of all the people who could have been the next guest on the Stern Show, that morning it was my former flame Lisa Lampanelli. Howard brought her in the studio and said, "You know you used to go out with this guy. You guys used to bang. Did you know he was gay?"

Lisa laughed about it and described sex with me.

"Awful, awful sex. Put it this way - he's a big fat bastard. I was hugely fat too man. And at 300 pounds, a guy who drops Howard Stern's name is hot to me, even if it is Joey Boots. The guy convinced me he was somebody dude. Cause I'm struggling doing $20 spots at the Comic Strip and this douchebag comes up saying, 'Hey maybe I could get you on Howard Stern.'"

Lisa used to have this joke that after she went out with me, she only dated black guys. So now I could say that Lisa drove me to like guys.

Only one person in my life reacted negatively to me coming out. It was this guy Buddy GZ who I used to do the greatest C-SPAN prank calls with. He hit me up on AOL Instant Messenger later that day and asked if that was real and if I was really gay. When I told him yeah, he signed off AIM, blocked me and took down all of our YouTube prank videos. I was kind of pissed about that because those were great clips. But overall, I couldn't have asked for a better response.

Even after all that, some in my life and on the show still didn't believe me. People like Artie Lange and others just thought it was a publicity stunt to get airtime or a prank like the ones I'd done before.

So two weeks later, Howard invited me back on the show to prove my gayness. They brought in this hot gay porn star Jason Ridge. Howard said if I was gay, I should make out with Jason and prove it to the world. No problem. I'd done a lot more with much worse looking guys.

We sat on the plush red Stern Show studio couch and enjoyed an extremely passionate kiss. Well at least I enjoyed it and Jason Ridge looked like he was having fun. It was really hot and passionate. I grabbed his package. A lot of hot tongue action. And when we were done, I went back again for seconds and started all over again. Yeah, it was beautiful.

The scene made some of the guys in the studio like Artie squeamish. But they believed me after that.

I liked Lisa and the other girls I banged, and it was fun. But it wasn't cerebral man. I wasn't attracted to her like I'm attracted to a guy. When I walk down the street, there might be a hot woman holding some guy's hand, and I'm checking out the hot guy.

CRAPTACULAR
INTERLUDE

During one of High Pitch Eric's Stern Show appearances, he was dressed in just a thong and doing some kind of stunt. Howard commented about how fat he was, and wondered how much Eric must shit each day after eating so much. That was the inspiration for the original Craptacular.

For that, the Howard TV crew spent the weekend at High Pitch's apartment to see how many pounds of waste he produced in 48 hours. He ate a lot and shit a lot.

Well I wanted in on the action. So I called into Howard and challenged Eric to a Craptacular face-off. I thought it would be funny. Plus my time spent in jail and the army had removed any qualms I had about shitting in public. And I was pretty high.

After a few times bugging them about it, they relented and organized the Craptacular 2. They even got a sponsor to throw in $5,000 to the winner whose shit weighed more after 48 hours.

So Howard TV brought a camera crew down to my apartment. Shuli was there reporting for Howard 100 News. Engineer Jim McClure was there. They also brought in an official looking shit-weighing lady who brought in two large scales.

We were neck and neck the first day. Then I pulled ahead. Mine weighed 1 pound and 7 ounces. Eric had just 23 ounces. Artie Lange bet money on Eric and began yelling, "You suck Eric! You can't even shit good!" Howard and Robin bet on Boots. High Pitch's stomach was killing him but he kept going. He produced another 12 ounces to pull even.

We were still so close and heading for a photo finish. Then with a half hour left, Eric pulled ahead with 1 pound 10 ounces. In the final moments, I evened the score again. Then Eric ate some of the fried calamari that I brought.

In the last minute, Eric squeezed a little bit more out and beat me by a few ounces. High Pitch was declared the undisputed, undefeated Craptacular champion.

Eric ended up splitting his prize cash with me and Artie gave us both the money he won gambling on High Pitch. Really everyone was a winner, except maybe the Howard TV crew. I've never seen people so grossed out and ready to puke. And you thought your job was shitty!

CHAPTER 24

CRASHED AND CRUSHED

Not long after the Craptacular, my life got really - well - crappy.

I was still doing lots of drugs. Sniffing coke, smoking crack, not to mention smoking weed and drinking as much if not more than ever. I was popping pills all the time, drinking every single day. Drinking easily over a case of beer a day.

I wasn't the guy who could sit there at a bar, have two drinks and be happy. I would want to keep drinking. And on my way home I'd wanna pick up beers to take home with me. And it wouldn't just be a six-pack of Tall Boys. It would be two six-packs of Tall Boys. Cause I didn't want to run out. I had that alarm going off in my head that I couldn't ever run out.

Eventually, it started to dawn on me that this drug life has gotta end or it would be over for me. End of the story.

So I was like let me move back to Miami where I had a support group of people. That was where I went for my first rehab that actually worked for a few months. I still kept in contact with a lot of people down there. So I packed up all my stuff and drove down to Miami to get off coke.

But I lasted about 17 days down there. I hated it. I felt myself getting back into drugs even when I was there in rehab. I didn't know as many people as I thought I would, and the people I did know had busier lives now and no time for me. I was sharing an apartment with some other guy in the program that I didn't know. I wasn't happy with where I was living or who I was living with. It was just going to meetings and that was it. I had no other life beyond that. It just sucked down there.

Shuli reported on Howard 100 News that I was miserable in Miami. How I just wanted to come back to New York but gave up my apartment and had nowhere to go. Then this guy Spencer, a Stern fan from New Jersey, contacted Shuli and said I could stay at his house while I got sober and situated back in the New York area. Spencer was a stockbroker and lived just outside the city. He said he was a recovering addict too and was going to meetings. He'd been sober for a while and we could get clean together. So I went to stay at his place.

Dude, within a week of me being there, Spencer started offering me his pain pills like Oxycodone. With no control,

I just accepted and started taking those pills that week. Then after another week he said, "Hey, I'm going out for some heroin. You want me to get you some?" I gave him $100 to get me a bundle - 10 packs of heroin. He came back with the drugs then left to go out for the night.

I had already been drinking vodka and Gatorade (a drink I called "Vatorade") and consumed a lot of Oxycodone throughout the day. And then I sniffed a bag of heroin. That was the last thing I remembered.

I woke up in an ambulance with paddles hitting my chest. I was being pumped full of the opiate blocker Narcan. My heart had stopped man. My heart stopped. I jumped up and the paramedics quickly said, "We're not the police, we're not the police. What did you take?"

I told them all the drugs I took. It turned out Spencer came home early. He saw me on the couch, and when he couldn't wake me up called an ambulance. Had he not come home early I'd have been dead.

Later that year, I was driving back from hanging with my friend Patrick in Eastchester. I had just been telling him how good it felt to be sober. That's what I was telling everyone. Patrick was taking me to lunch to celebrate where I was in life.

But while I was driving home I was smoking crack. I was flying man, doing like 90 mph on the Bronx River Parkway, which has some really narrow sections. And I was smoking crack while driving. High as fuck man.

I was in the fast lane when suddenly my car spun out, hit the median and ended up facing the wrong way in traffic. Thank God there were no other cars coming dude since this was mid-afternoon. I was able to turn my car around and get off the exit in Yonkers. The whole front end was hanging off. There was a cop directing traffic by the exit and he was signaling for me to go left. Then the cop saw my fucked-up car, and started motioning for me to pull over. But I just kept going. I ditched my car a few blocks up and reported it stolen. I was afraid. I was so high.

I was a serious crack addict.

After that, I went to a rehab run by monks in upstate NY called Saint Christopher's Inn. The Franciscan Friars of the Atonement were dedicated to the rehabilitation of men in crisis. The men who needed help were called Brothers Christopher. I was up there for 72 days.

And that place really worked well for me. At Saint Christopher's Inn, I was away from the city, drugs and people with drugs. It was as simple as that. Not having access to those vices. I went to meetings, took classes on how to stay sober and had lots of counseling. But the biggest thing was the isolation. It was also more spiritual a place than anywhere I'd ever been. It was a really good place and I was clean the entire time.

When you're away from the drugs and people, it's easier to stay sober. And you can talk the game. You can even think you want to stay sober. But when you hit the real world again, that's where the trial starts.

The day after I left Saint Christopher's Inn, I moved into a sober home in Yonkers so the counselors there could help with the transition. Then I came out to Long Island and paid a short visit to my parents and other family, assuring them all I would live a clean and simple life. After that, I went right to my dealer and hooked up. I bought some crack off him.

I left the sober home when the counselors gave me their stamp of sober approval. In addition to being a drug abuser, like a lot of addicts I had become a talented trust abuser.

I found an apartment on West 51st street in Hell's Kitchen. It was a 5-story apartment building that was basically a flophouse. You rented a private room then shared a bathroom and shower with people on your floor. But it didn't matter because it was cool having a place in Manhattan and I wanted to make a fresh start. And that area of the city was becoming a lot more gay. So I was thinking I could finally find a boyfriend somewhere.

On my first day there, I became fast friends with a guy in the building named Downey. He was a big fan of the Howard Stern Show and knew my name and voice from there. He even appeared occasionally on the "Superfan Roundtable" – a weekly show on the Howard 101 Sirius channel.

Downey was selling coke and morphine pills out of his room. He had a big jar of like 500 morphine pills, which I was popping with him throughout the day.

That first night, I'd been up all night in Downey's room using his computer. It was about 5 a.m. when suddenly the door flew open and a whole police raid team stormed in with shields and helmets and dogs and guns. The cops slammed me down on the bed and put a gun to my head. They rousted Downey out of sleep and hauled us off to jail man.

Dude, the very first night living there I got arrested.

The cops said the building inspector smelled marijuana coming out of the room, which I think was bullshit. Someone who bought weed from Downey probably got busted and ratted him out in exchange for leniency from the police.

This was my first day out of the sober home. I was supposed to be making a fresh start.

We spent over 12 hours in the tombs below the criminal court building in lower Manhattan. I got up in front of a judge at about midnight with a misdemeanor charge of possession. The District Attorney asked for $5,000 bail. But the judge denied bail and released me on my own recognizance.

Downey was facing some serious felonies because in addition to weed, he had a lot of coke on him. But he also got released on his own recognizance. I guess we were both pretty recognizable.

Because I was arrested on my first night as a tenant, my new West 51st street landlord evicted me right away. Downey could stay in his place because he'd been living there for years. In New York if it's been less than a year, the landlord can evict you with fewer legal hurdles. Downey invited me to crash with him. So I ended up doing that. I went back and stayed with him, sleeping on the floor of his small room. Doing drugs every day.

Even though the cops confiscated all of his drugs, Downey replenished quickly. The first couple days at his place I started doing drugs again, mostly coke.

But then I was like you know what man? I gotta stop. It's done. So I started going to meetings again and started trying to get back to my normal life. Even trying to figure out what a normal life was, because I was pretty sure I never experienced it.

I just knew I had to get out of that apartment. I told Downey I couldn't stay there anymore. So I moved, and nobody knew this, but I went out and stayed with Shuli and his wife Christine in Queens. They just wanted me to get the hell out of Downey's apartment and away from bad influences.

Shuli and Christine saved my life man. They got me out of there. Christine was pregnant. It was so nice of them to take me in. They trusted that I wasn't gonna be a problem or relapse again there. I love them to death and I'm so grateful. They saved my life man and got me out of that environment. I was going to meetings and finally feeling some clarity.

And then I went back to that apartment and talked to Downey about checking himself into a hospital so he could get clean too. And I said, "Listen, I can take you to Bellevue Hospital. You can go to detox and you can get off this shit. I think maybe you should start a new life. Living a good life. Living a righteous life. Living the good life you deserve to live. And just leave all this other shit behind."

Downey reflected on this for a few moments. "Yeah man… Yeah, I'll go tomorrow."

But then the next day came and he was still partying. And he said, "I'll get help later." Then later turned into the next day. Then he said, "Let me go Monday." And I said, "Listen dude, I know what you want to do. You wanna party your brains out one last weekend and say goodbye to your drugs. I did it before. I understand. But it's not necessarily a good thing. A lot of people don't come back from that."

So I went to get Downey on Monday and take him to detox. I was ready to help but expected more delays. Either way, I was gonna support my friend.

But when I got there, the building manager was standing by the front entrance. "You can't go in there, Joey. Downey's dead."

It turned out Downey's mother in Florida couldn't reach him on his phone, so she called the building manager and asked him to check on her son. His door was unlocked, so the manager opened it and found him dead in his bed. He OD'd.

This shocked and horrified me and I was just standing there stunned on the street. Processing. Speechless.

Just then, Howard 100 News reporter Steve Langford jumped out from behind a car and put his microphone in my face. Langford peppered me with questions about Downey and what happened. The building manager had called and notified him. He knew Steve because High Pitch Eric lived in the same building before, and the manager was a big Howard Stern fan.

Downey's mom was in Florida, so she needed someone in New York to go identify his body so they could release him for burial. First she asked Steve Langford to do it, but he called and pleaded for me to go instead.

So I went to the morgue on First Avenue - the NYC Medical Examiner's office. I did it for his mother and for Downey. I felt really bad. I went with Harry, another friend of mine from the building who also knew and loved Downey. We saw him and both started crying. We hugged each other.

That was really hard for me to see and do that. My friend didn't make it man. A couple weeks later, I packed up his belongings and sent them home.

So that happened.

CHAPTER 25

AFTERMATH

I went right to a meeting after that and haven't stopped going since. They say every addict hits that bottom. To see a guy who you were just hanging out and bullshitting with lying on a slab motionless, never taking a breath of life again. Oh, it was horrible man. And all because of drugs and the bad decisions that come from drugs. And it could have been me a million times.

I started going to meetings a few times a week in lower Manhattan. I don't want to say what kinds of meetings, because the group I belong to has a certain tradition of anonymity. Then I checked myself in to a long-term rehab for 5 months up in Western New York run by the VA. I decided to go up there to reinforce everything I needed to know and do to make this work. And that rehab pretty much did it for me man. Since then I've been clean and sober. I just needed some more time away. I got sick and tired of being sick and tired. I wanted to live.

Since coming back from that rehab, I've been refocusing on contributing to the world of entertainment, mostly by shooting street videos. At least once or twice a month my clips have gone viral or made national and international news. People love my videos and I've licensed quite a few of them to news organizations. On one of my clips I even made 5-figures. And I'm a medically retired military, so I also get income from a pension.

I've had a few YouTube channels, some of which have been shut down for going against their decency standards. So I'm always trying to find new places to post clips. A lot are controversial.

I engage interesting and unique individuals throughout NYC in conversation. That person you might pass on the street and never think of talking to, I'll stop them. Or that guy with his finger up his butt talking to a fire hydrant. I'll go up to that person, start talking to him and record it on my flip cam.

I've been attacked a few times while shooting video. People come up and punch me, try to knock the camera out of my hands and spit on me. But all I think about is how great this video is gonna be. Later when I walk away and review the footage I think damn I could have really gotten hurt there.

In no way am I trying to take advantage of people. I try to show them as human beings. Find out their problems, how they got where they are and ask if there's anything they need. I give a lot to the homeless and do whatever I can for them.

The *Village Voice* newspaper recently named me "Citizen of the Week." This was after my film footage helped police arrest a shoplifter. I was able to get the suspect's license plate before he sped off. He turned out to be an off-duty NYC firefighter.

But the last time the *Village Voice* wrote about me, they labeled me "Joey Boots Asshole." They called me that for shouting negative things at politicians attending that tax cheat Rep. Charlie Rangel's birthday party.

Going from asshole to hero? I'll take that.

I also still occasionally go back to my roots by interrupting live reporters on the street shouting "Baba Booey" or "Howard Stern's penis." That never gets old.

I recently did a Booey Bomb in Union Square during a newscast and got arrested by a cop for disorderly conduct. They offered a plea deal, but I refused and took the case to trial. The judge said what I did was perfectly legal and that "Baba Booey" and "Howard Stern's penis" are protected free speech, because no obscenity laws were violated. He said it was just like sports fans shouting team names. So long live the Booey Bomb. You should try it sometime.

I just interviewed Howard Stern outside the *America's Got Talent* auditions at Radio City. He became a new judge on *AGT* and they moved the whole show to New York for him. When Howard saw me with my camera amidst a sea of media and fans, he said, "Hey, Joey dude. Joey Boots is a wise man." And that made me feel good and look good to everyone around. Howard was real nice to me.

The other day I interviewed Tucker Carlson while he was fly fishing in Central Park. Then Russell Simmons down at Occupy Wall Street. "You're Joey Boots?" Russell asked. "You're famous!"

I just got my first role in a feature film. *Being Flynn* starring Robert De Niro, based on the 2006 novel *Another Bullshit Night in Suck City* by Nick Flynn. As I was walking to the audition, my pants accidentally got caught on my foot and ripped all the way up to my ass. So my skimpy underwear with holes was exposed from the back, and I didn't have time to run home and change.

So when I got in the audition room, the first thing I did was turn around and show my exposed ass. I apologized and told them what happened. The whole room busted out laughing. That was what convinced director Paul Weitz to cast me. It's a small role. I play a Narcotics Anonymous drug counselor and have 2 scenes.

I see a shrink every week at the VA hospital. It's good man, it's healthy. The people I'm around now are all different. I don't hang out with knuckleheads anymore. I hang out with winners. People living lives that I want to emulate.

And I now have a relationship with my family beyond my wildest dreams. My parents, two brothers, sisters-in-law, nieces and nephews. I'm able to be a son, a brother and an uncle. I'm able to show up, be there and do things for them and not cause any more pain. I try not to cause anybody pain in my life anymore.

And that's how I start my day man. I meditate in the morning. And part of that meditation is asking that I not cause anybody any pain today.

I finally accepted that I really can't just have one drink. There's a saying in rehab that the first drink is too much, and a thousand is never enough. My main motivation for staying clean is that I'm feeling spiritual now man. I knew that there was nothing on this Earth that was gonna keep me sober other than finding it in myself.

I still see Shuli sometimes. We don't hang out as much, because he and his wife have a baby now. But they're real proud of all the positive changes and progress I've made. We still talk a lot on the phone. With him still being a Howard 100 News reporter, Shuli does reports on my antics that keep me relevant. Just a few weeks ago, I stayed at his house dog-sitting while he and his family were vacationing in Vegas. It meant a lot to me that they would trust me by myself in their home after what happened in my past.

I now live in the same apartment building as High Pitch Eric – so I have a celebrity neighbor. We live in the Bronx just two floors apart from each other. Now I can go over there and ask for some powder – sugar for my coffee of course! High Pitch works at the Yankee Stadium Hard Rock Café as a greeter. Stern fans go there and take pictures with him. Hi daddy!

I hang out with Eric a lot, sometimes going to all-you-can-eat Chinese buffets to the dismay of the proprietors, who shake their heads as we take multiple heaping plates of food.

Eric and I have both gotten extremely fat. When I stopped drinking and drugging, I started eating a lot. Pizza, fried chicken, soda, ice cream and more pizza. I was already overweight and in the last year and a half gained 90 more pounds. Why couldn't I get addicted to being healthy and going to the gym? It just didn't comfort me as much at the time. Food comforted me you know? It did and now I'm ashamed of myself because I'm fat. But I still give killer blowjobs.

I'm still seeking a boyfriend. I've never had a boyfriend and that hasn't changed since I came out. Maybe my future boyfriend is reading this. Someone funny, somebody cute. I'm available. Hit me up @JoeyBoots.

My Twitter account was suspended for a while, I think because of malicious complaints. But then I went to the CEO's house on Long Island and left a handwritten note in his mailbox. My account was soon restored, and verified with that blue check this time.

So has being part of the Howard Stern Show had a positive or negative impact on my life?

I think it was mostly positive man. Howard and the show gave me access to a really cool life. I met lots of great people, did a lot of fun things and it gave me some notoriety and recognition that I so craved all my life. I was always an unpopular kid in school so I fed off of that attention.

There were also negative influences that spawned from my experiences there. But do I blame the show? I have nobody to blame but me for putting myself in any kind of position that I was in. Like out in Vegas doing all sorts of drugs. Hanging out with Beetlejuice doing all sorts of drugs, hanging with other people doing all sorts of drugs. In short, I was doing all sorts of drugs. I don't know if you've picked up on that yet.

Maybe there were times I demoralized myself like the Icy Hot stunt and Craptacular. But I'm really not ashamed of anything. What wasn't great was that when they launched the uncensored Howard TV On-Demand channel, the Icy Hot stunt was one of the first shows they ran. But this time they removed the blurry pixilation from my crotch. So my small penis was exposed to the world uncensored. Because of that, I'm never gonna run for president. It's not really a small penis - it's just at that moment it was small. Please do not look up and view that video.

So no weed, no pills, no alcohol, it's a sober life man.

Can I do this forever? I can do it today. I'm not gonna project into the future man. I have faith that in the future, should I keep doing what I'm doing now, I'll stay sober. I can never tell you what's gonna happen tomorrow. But I can tell you right now that I'm sober. Today I'm sober.

And I can't dwell too much on the past either. I'm not gonna forget, but I'm not gonna dwell on it too much. A lot of the past was the foundation to be where I am today. That's where I'm at right now man. I'm at a good place in my head. I think I'm on a good path. I'm living a righteous life. Doing good, creative things. Full of love for my family and friends, and they love me. And I'm actually taking suggestions from people who are living a good life as opposed to just letting myself run the show.

So much different from a few years ago man. So much different.

There's always the fear you're gonna relapse again. And hey, should I relapse, I know that I can come right back to the open arms of people I love and get in the program. There's no, "Ha-ha he went out, he got high." No it's not like that man. Cause there's so many people who never do return. And then wind up dying out there because they're too ashamed and embarrassed. But I'm not. I know that if I come back, it will be to loving arms. People saying welcome back. We love you.

We're so glad you made it back.

THE LAST CHRONICLE

This time, Joey Boots didn't make it back.

On December 23, 2016, Joey didn't show up to host his weekly podcast, "The Joey Boots Show," on the Podtrash website. His cohost Gonzo Shitcock texted High Pitch Eric, who lived two floors below, and asked if he could go upstairs and check on his friend. At first Eric said no, but Gonzo bribed him with the promise of a future pizza.

High Pitch went up, knocked on the door, and no one answered. Then he called Joey's cell phone and was able to hear ringing from the other side. But still no answer or response. Eric asked the building manager to unlock the door and do a wellness check.

They opened the door and discovered him sitting in a chair by his desk in front of his computer, slumped over.

He had no pulse and his body was ice cold. Joey Boots was dead.

As the building manager and emergency services dealt with the scene, Eric called into the podcast to say what happened. At first, cohosts Gonzo and Chad from St. Louis thought it was a prank. But it soon became apparent that this was no joke. A beloved member of the Stern Show universe was gone.

Right away, drug rumors began circulating among fans, because Joey had been open about his past addiction and relapses. But his close friends including High Pitch insisted he'd been sober at the time. The NYPD said there were no visible signs of trauma, and appeared to be natural causes.

On March 13th, TMZ.com reported that the New York Medical Examiner determined it was "acute heroin intoxication." An accidental heroin overdose.

Besides TMZ, news of the death and the discovery of the cause was reported by the *New York Post*, *People Magazine*, *Fox News*, *Daily News*, *Drudge Report*, *Chicago Tribune*, *Daily Beast*, *Entertainment Weekly* and the UK's *Daily Mail* and trended in the Twitter top 10.

Do you think Joey would have at least appreciated this publicity? A few headlines called him "Joey Boots Baba Booey."

Some TV news shows equated this with other tragic celebrity deaths of 2016 including David Bowie, Prince and George Michael. Reporters who'd been Booey Bombed by him in the past spoke fondly of the incidents. They said that while these disturbances were annoying at the time, they became humorous in retrospect. And by being on the Howard Stern Show, even for a prank, they too gained national exposure. Howard later noted that the people he harassed most were now the most reverential.

Stern fans across social media lamented. The loss came during a string of Wack Pack-related deaths. Crackhead Bob, Eric the Actor and Riley Martin were all lost recently. Then Nicole Bass a few weeks later.

When this happened, the show was on Christmas vacation. But Howard tweeted:

@HowardStern 24 Dec 2016
Tribute to the one and only Joey B in the new year.
He will be missed. #BababooeyHowardSternspenis

And on the morning they returned, the Joey Boots Tribute lasted over an hour with no commercial breaks.

Howard started by saying that when he found out, he broke the news to talk show host and superfan Jimmy Kimmel. They wondered if High Pitch Eric and Joey were like Carrie Fisher and Debbie Reynolds. That if one went, the other would be dead within hours. Since Kimmel was hosting the Oscars soon, Howard said they should include Joey in the "In Memoriam" segment because of his *Being Flynn* film role.

Howard and Robin Quivers discussed whether or not he was a member of the Wack Pack.

"It was always kind of debatable if Joey was considered a Wack Packer," Howard said. "Because I could sit down with Joey off the air and actually have a normal conversation with him. He wasn't that crazy. And in order to be in the Wack Pack, you have to be really fucking out of your mind. Or half-human, half-retarded. But he was kind of a normal guy in a weird way."

Robin agreed, "He liked to do crazy things, but he wasn't crazy."

They played musical tributes sent in by fans and clips of Joey's memorable show moments like the Craptacular and when he came out. They played classic Booey Bombs. Howard's favorite was Fox News on New Year's Eve. There was so much yelling behind the reporter that she was oblivious to Joey. So he was able to shout "Baba Booey" and "Howard Stern's Penis" multiple times without interruption.

Howard brought High Pitch Eric into the studio. Eric said, through tears, that the tribute was great so far. "When I came in this morning, I said damn, Joey's not here with me today. I'm going to miss you from the bottom of my heart. I love you. You are always going to be with me forever and ever."

So what were Joey Boots' contributions to the world, and did these contributions benefit society? Decide from these pages, YouTube, and the thoughts of others who may have different perspectives on these chronicles. But it was a unique life.

Howard Stern said, "Joey had a hard life, but he told us a lot of things brought him joy, and one of them was our show. I liked Joey very, very much and I'm going to miss him very much. He was a great friend to the show.

"He more than anyone got the name Howard Stern Show out. 'Howard Stern's Penis' and 'Baba Booey.' And it always made for a great laugh. And he did it for the show. And it was very nice of him, very kind of him. And I always loved when he would call in or come in to the show.

"So I am gonna miss the Joey Boots who would take his fingers and apply ass cream to High Pitch Eric, and all of these different stories. He's a good character, he's a good guy. Joey Boots - we speak your name."

55164564R00128

Made in the USA
Middletown, DE
15 July 2019